THE ROCK CARLING FELLOWSHIP

1980

Professional or public health?

SOCIOLOGY IN HEALTH
AND MEDICINE

THE ROCK CARLING FELLOWSHIP

1980

PROFESSIONAL OR PUBLIC HEALTH?

SOCIOLOGY IN HEALTH AND MEDICINE

Raymond Illsley

CBE, BA, PhD

*Director, MRC Medical Sociology Unit
and Professor of Medical Sociology
University of Aberdeen*

THE NUFFIELD PROVINCIAL
HOSPITALS TRUST
1980

Published by the
Nuffield Provincial Hospitals Trust
3 Prince Albert Road, London NW1 7SP

ISBN 0 900574 33 X
© Nuffield Provincial Hospitals Trust, 1980

Designed by Bernard Crossland
PRINTED IN GREAT BRITAIN BY
BURGESS & SON (ABINGDON) LTD
ABINGDON OXFORDSHIRE

CONTENTS

vii

Contents

PREFACE

I have never been taught sociology. At the University I read modern history but never got past the eighteenth century, and returned after the war to study economics, with a compulsory nod to politics and philosophy. My first article (fortunately anonymous) as an economic assistant dealt with the hen population of Poland—good training perhaps for my later demographic work on pregnancy in Aberdeen. In my second job as a social and economic officer to a New Town I first learnt what a big gap existed between research and its implementation. On my way from Sussex to Aberdeen to be interviewed for a job as a 'social scientist' with Dugald Baird's Department of Midwifery, I hurriedly read Douglas' *Maternity in Great Britain*. It was my first contact with either medicine, epidemiology, or sociology. As a radical student I had read Marx but thought of him as a political philosopher, and a deviant economist, being unaware that sociologists had adopted him as one of their founding fathers. For many years I felt embarrassed, a bit of a fraud, in the presence of my true sociological colleagues as they discussed Weber, Durkheim, or Simmel with all the familiarity of old personal friends. This was not an unusual history for a sociologist in the 1950s. Few had been trained (few were wanted) and many, like myself, graduated, crab-wise, into our discipline from odd starting points.

There was no Department of Sociology in Aberdeen, there were no sociologists, and I learnt my trade from an obstetrician, Dugald Baird, and an epidemiologist, Angus Thomson, to both of whom I owe a large and continuing debt of gratitude. Perhaps they knew no more about sociology than I did, but they had clear ideas about scientific method, a respect for first-hand data and an insight into the potential contribution of the social sciences to medicine—and especially to the understanding of how life-styles might affect mortality and morbidity in pregnancy and childbirth. They, and Jerry Morris who supported the

Preface

Aberdeen research team from his London-based MRC unit, were as unusual in the Medical Schools of that time as was my presence in medical research. On the way to my desk in the old forensic medicine museum, I was often met, in the nicest possible way, by the head of a neighbouring Department, with the greeting, 'Well, Illsley, how's social welfare today?'—a question I never learnt to handle.

Medical sociology got invented sometime in the 1950s, I became a proper sociologist (still a bit vague about the founding fathers) and have continued to live between the two worlds of medicine and sociology. Inter-disciplinary research is always difficult to achieve and even more difficult to sustain on a long-term basis. A fellow-sociologist, convinced that sociology could only suffer and be seduced from its true path by close association with medicine, presented me, in the early years of the MRC Medical Sociology Unit, with an offprint entitled something like 'Storm in a prairie dust-bowl'. It described the brief rise and fall in Mid-West America of a research institute committed to inter-disciplinary research. The institute started with a clear problem which demanded contributions from several disciplines. It neared its first goal and received considerable acclaim. Thereafter, as each disciplinary participant got deeper into his field secondary objectives, specific to each discipline, took over, the common aims disappeared in a dust-cloud of scientific disputation and the institute disintegrated. In writing this book I have become very conscious that my initial task of documenting and explaining the relationship between life-styles and mortality and morbidity in pregnancy was at least partially lost in the development of medical sociology as a discipline. It seemed so important to follow-up suggestive findings on social mobility, on migration, and later on child upbringing and to explore their sociological ramifications that ultimately the Unit ended up studying alcoholism and geriatrics.

The process could be explained as a personality aberration (and perhaps with some degree of truth) but there were more fundamental influences which affect all inter-disciplinary work. My colleagues in obstetrics were simultaneously following their disciplinary pathways into metabolism, hypertension, and other bio-medical phenomena which took them back into their

x

laboratories and away from the original common task. The division of the scientific world into specialisms centres each of us upon certain concepts and paradigms which can occasionally be made to coincide by the special features of a practical problem, by charismatic leadership, and sometimes by the availability of research funds. But because their boundaries differ, further exploration of each concept produces centrifugal movement. The study of life-styles, for example, can only with difficulty be concentrated permanently upon pregnant women; it quickly raises questions about antecedents in childhood and adolescence, manifestations in later adult life and in the features of social structure which produce and sustain differences in life-styles. When I was approached in the late 1950s by two highly innovative American research workers, Dr Herbert Birch and Dr Stephen Richardson, who themselves combined sociology, psychology, paediatrics, and neurology in their perspectives and who were asking penetrating questions about these very issues, I was ready for a switch in perspectives.

External developments in a discipline also exert strong pressures and perhaps this is particularly the case with a young, thrusting, iconoclastic subject making its debut on the scientific scene. Sociology was expanding rapidly all over the Western World in the 1960s and its focus was very different from that which had developed in an epidemiologically-oriented Department of Obstetrics. Medical sociology shared in that growth but elsewhere it was concentrated fairly strongly on those medical problems— and particularly problems of mental health—directly concerned with behavioural questions. The concepts which excited new recruits into medical sociology were those of deviance, labelling, conflict, and the ideological assumptions of medicine about human behaviour. In obstetrics, too, interest had shifted to family planning, abortion, sterilization, and population growth. Under these two pressures the centre of interest changed from the study of individuals in their social environment to the study of the professions and of the practice of medicine. How were decisions reached? How far, for example, did decisions about abortion reflect medical-scientific criteria and how far were they value-decisions based on current ideologies in the profession and society

xi

at large? Very similar questions were posed about psychiatric treatment, particularly in those conditions such as neurosis, depression, or alcoholism where definition of the condition itself was highly problematic and variable. At a later period changes within sociology and within the health services began to raise questions about health policy and the organization of services which sociologists could not avoid and which brought a further widening in the interests and scope of medical sociology.

Most medical specialties are linked to a clinical practice. New scientific developments may tempt them down exciting research pathways but ultimately they are brought back to the treatment of a defined group of patients, or diseases, and to the organization of a service. Medical sociology does not have that everyday anchor. Its boundaries are neither medicine nor health in the conventional sense, because it cannot ignore the social environment which produces patients, nor the contiguous social services which interact with both doctors and patients. It is therefore necessarily a more theoretical discipline in which ideas and concepts take the place of patients and diseases as their permanent concern and the framework within which research is formulated. Such concepts as decision-making, deviance, or disability are the central foci of theory and of empirical research and they stretch across the clinical and administrative boundaries which medicine has evolved for treatment purposes. It is therefore logical, if somewhat tiring, for a sociologist to pursue some central conceptual interest across paediatrics, psychiatry, geriatrics, and health policy. His objectives will be different from those of each of the clinicians he meets on the way. When agreeing to co-operate in joint research with a medical group, I usually find it worthwhile to define explicitly our common and our separate interests and to emphasize that the latter do not always coincide.

Given these difficulties, it is, I think, remarkable that medical sociology has found such a firm place within medical research and that so much co-operation takes place, with varying degrees of mutual satisfaction, between two such different disciplines. We still meet today's equivalent of 'how's social welfare today?' and sociologists are still tempted into substituting 'doctor-bashing' for scientific enquiry. The foundations have been laid, however, for fruitful relationships and I, for one, still find excitement in pursuing our common, parallel, diverging, and converging research activities.

I have tried throughout the book to give some idea of the scope of medical sociology and of its distinctive perspectives on health and medicine. Whilst, therefore, much of the text is descriptive I have also taken the opportunity to air my own views. I am, for example, critical of the processes by which health policy is formulated, and of the way in which a professionally-dominated service equates public health with professional health. I have described the inescapable methodological problems intrinsic to the study of social relations and defended sociology against the conventional charges of subjectivity and lack of methodological rigour. Indeed I suggest that, in the study of health services and of policy formulation and implementation, the application of sociological methods is long over-due. Whilst not unhappy about the state of medical sociology compared with a decade or more ago, I am sceptical about the adequacy of arrangements for graduate education and for the training of research workers. I am also doubtful whether the present ad hoc arrangements for funding and organization of research through the University sector are appropriate for producing research of the type and quality required for further development of the subject and for successful application to current health and health service problems.

Mains of Kebbaty
Midmar
Aberdeenshire

July 1980

ACKNOWLEDGEMENTS

Many people have contributed to this book. I wish to thank the many past and present members of the MRC Medical Sociology Unit whose works I have quoted so frequently. Mildred Blaxter, Graeme Ford, Marion Hall, and Gordon Horobin each made valuable comments on sections of the script. I owe special thanks to Barbara Thompson, not only for her help with ideas and data but for her constant support over many years as colleagues in research. Rex Taylor read every word of the script, changed many of them, and was so constructive in his criticism that the better passages are more likely to be his than mine. Howard Kelman of Stony Brook University, New York, has spent many hours over many years discussing with me the methodological problems raised by the study of dependency groups. Anne Forbes typed the whole manuscript, more than once, with her usual cool competence and patience. My wife, Jean, supported me throughout the writing of this book as she has throughout my research life.

I

Introduction

A healthy woman visits her general practitioner for confirmation
of pregnancy, begins to talk about marital problems, the stress of
bringing up her existing children, and doing a full-time job, and
eventually leaves the surgery with a referral to the gynaecological out-patient department for consideration of termination
of pregnancy.... A patient treated for a severe accident at work
is discharged with a residual handicap and returns home to
reconstruct his life with whatever assistance he can mobilize
from his GP, his employer, the disablement rehabilitation service,
the local social security office, the social work department, and his
network of family and friends.... A group of clinical psychologists evolve new methods of handling senile dementia and begin a
series of negotiations to obtain patients and professional freedom
to apply their techniques .... A local Health Board decides to
convert a local maternity hospital into a geriatric unit and runs
into a storm of professional and lay criticism .... The DHSS
issues guidelines calling for a reduction in drug use and a switch
of resources from hospital curative medicine to the care of the
chronic sick in the community. All these examples have several
common components. They all deal with the management of
patients and the exercise of medical knowledge and judgement.
They all touch on matters for which, at the clinical level, medical
doctors are responsible and accountable and they all involve the
use of health service manpower and resources. On the other hand
they do not all relate to medically-defined illness. The pregnant
mother is experiencing a normal physiological process and the
decision to refer her for a possible abortion requires the use of
knowledge and judgements about marital and family life and the
application of values about what is morally and socially acceptable behaviour. Had she become pregnant last year, whilst still
living in Birmingham rather than Newcastle or Aberdeen, the
outcome might well have been different. The disabled worker

cannot benefit from further surgical or orthopaedic skills and is discharged home to deal with the aftermath of illness and the difficulties of mobilizing a set of separate professional and bureaucratic organizations and getting them to adapt their procedures and regulations to his requirements. Some hospital departments and some general practitioners will see it as their medical responsibility to co-ordinate rehabilitative services on his behalf, but others interpret their medical-professional roles more strictly and leave him to chart his own way through the administrative jungle. The clinical psychologists are undoubtedly dealing with medically-defined illness, and given our present inability to manage senile dementia patients effectively and humanely, their techniques might well be an improvement on what now happens. The essential issues here stem from the legal and administrative accountability of physicians for their patients, the problems posed by professional boundaries, and the constraints experienced by young and proselytizing disciplines attempting to enter occupied territory. The Health Board, attempting to change the use of hospital buildings in the interests of rationalization and the more economic use of resources, accepts its own responsibility and those of its medical staff for the care and treatment of both maternity and geriatric patients, but runs into intra-professional conflict within medicine. It is also confronted with delicate problems of local democracy and competing judgements about who is best fitted to determine the balance of health needs and resources in the community it serves. All these issues, from the effectiveness and efficiency of medical treatment, the appropriate division of medical and non-medical labour, the economic use of limited resources between competing ends to ideas about the locus of decision-making, are confronted by the DHSS in its issue of guidelines.

For the sociologist these examples have other common components. They are all examples of health-related events, each referring to medical responsibilities and treatment, where medical and social criteria are used in combination. In the first instance medical criteria concerning the decision to abort (as opposed to the performance of the operation) are used mainly as limiting conditions related to the safety of the operation and the viability of the foetus. The remaining criteria relate to the ethical and theological values of the physician or his conceptions of marital and family life and the welfare of social institutions. The second instance, that of rehabilitation after hospital treatment, is more complicated involving differing perceptions of the role of the physician and of the boundaries where medical treatment and responsibilities end. The third instance of clinical psychology and senile dementia is basically an issue of the division of labour and the hierarchy of professional autonomy. The remaining two examples refer to the economic use of resources, differing public and professional perceptions of social needs, and the role of national or local, public or professional bodies in decisions about social priorities.

These examples are professionally interesting to sociologists for many other reasons. The conduct of a medical consultation is a specific example of a process of social interaction which has its counterparts in many other areas of social and economic life. Interviews or consultations conducted by physicians, social workers, lawyers, or employers may differ in content but they are comparable in that they each involve an exchange of information, skills, and decisions and can be seen to have a common structure. An analysis by three general practitioners and an educationalist (Byrne and Long, 1976) of 2500 tape-recorded consultations distinguishes six phases of an interview: greeting and relating, discovering the reasons for attendance, conducting a verbal or physical examination or both, a consideration of the condition, detailing further treatment, and terminating the interviews. Most consultations will contain variants of these phases but they will differ in form and manner in patterned ways which, apart from the idiosyncratic personality characteristics of the participants, reflect the purpose of the consultation, its physical setting, the knowledge, education, and social status of the participants, their relative status and power in relationship to the service being requested and offered, and the degrees of judgement and discretion involved. Each phase has implications for inter-action at subsequent stages. Strong (1980) shows how it is standard procedure in American private practice for the physician to introduce himself by name (and even by qualifications) and to spend several minutes in establishing a social person-to-person relationship before broaching the reasons for attendance. This contrasts with the formal anonymity of out-patient paediatric consultations in the United Kingdom, observed by the same investigator. The passing of the Abortion Act and the general acceptance of abortion as responsible behaviour has changed the earlier hesitant flow of suggestion and innuendo, of implicit encouragement or overt discouragement into more direct question-and-answer and has given the patient greater power in the interaction. Sociologists are concerned mainly with social structure, social processes, and social relationships and the medical consultation is therefore intrinsically interesting to them as one example of the influence of structure and relationships on process. Consultation procedures, however, have clear consequences upon outcome (see the discussion of adenotonsillectomy in chapter 7 below) and therefore represent one area of mutual interest to both physicians and sociologists.

Specialization and the division of labour may stimulate sophisticated knowledge, high technology, and a greater output of better and cheaper production. Its inevitable social corollary is the sub-division of the work-force, whether in industry, commerce, government, or the professions, into groups with separate interests. The organization of these groups to further their interests may create an internal solidarity at the expense of external conflict. Putting the parts together requires the creation of co-ordinating agencies and the application of rules and procedures to regulate the relationships between groups, their share of the common task, and the hierarchy of authority both within and between them. The disabled worker on return from hospital may need help with problems of personal care, money, employment, and family relationships. He may find himself in difficulties, not merely because he is confused by the multiplicity of agencies created for his benefit, but also because each agency has adopted its own administrative criteria to determine who shall benefit and to what extent. Moreover, these criteria are often mutually contradictory and designed for the average case rather than the range of individual needs. After observing the subsequent history of 194 patients discharged from hospital with residual

4

impairment Blaxter (1976) commented that the rehabilitation system 'may seem to owe more to the requirements of institutional structures than to the original intentions'. Whilst the medical profession, and particularly general practice, had developed a one-to-one relationship with its clients, had learned that every patient is an individual, and had adapted to working in a context of uncertainty, other parts of the welfare system tended to work in dichotomous categories (a man is sick, or he is not: his injury is industrial or it is not: he is eligible for benefit or he is not) and could not tolerate uncertainties. These are issues primarily of the division of labour and of the sociology of organizations and for medical specialties and the health system the dilemma is how they should relate to other organizational structures whose operation can negate their own contribution.

The case of the clinical psychologists and the management of senile dementia is also a problem of boundary management. A new profession with distinctive skills is challenging established procedures and seeking the opportunity, within the health service structure, to apply its treatment methods to patients for whom the medical profession has ultimate accountability. Just over a decade ago, social workers occupied a similar marginal position, dependent upon medicine for the referral of patients whose problems might benefit from their skills. The 'professional' solution to their problem came with the integration of the social work profession across the various services to which they contributed and this enabled them to operate from an independent power base (it did not, however, solve the fundamental problem of how two professions might offer a co-ordinated service to patients). The psychologists' problem differs in that they are offering not a complementary service, but an alternative treatment and they, moreover, are unlikely to find an external power base from which to negotiate. Nurses and various other categories of therapists differ only in the degrees to which they have achieved professional autonomy at the clinical level and in the extent of their co-option into the managerial and planning system. Throughout the economic system negotiation between individuals jointly involved in a common enterprise has been and is being replaced by negotiation between organized groups. In the process deals are struck which are mutually acceptable to workers but in which consumers or third parties have no negotiating rights. The inter- and intra-professional rivalries of the health service are therefore but a single example of conflicts and contradictions endemic within a post-industrial society and, as such, they are the 'bread and butter' issues of sociology.

The two final examples also raise questions of authority and the right to make decisions. Like each of the other questions their origin lies in a combination of social change and technological advance. Sociologists, equally with medicine and other professions, differ from each other in their conceptualization of problems and speak with divided tongues. In general, however, they tend to see the health system as a major institution of all societies—comparable with the law, the church, the family, the defence system, or the form of government—'created' to serve societal ends, adapting itself to demographic and economic conditions, but containing elements of tradition and stability and defended by ideological principles which are resistant to both internal development and external pressures. The tensions between obstetrics and geriatrics, between cure and care, between hospital and community, between local interests and administrative rationalization, and between professional and public determination of the use of resources are merely a contemporary manifestation in one institutional structure of tensions which are endemic (some might say epidemic) in all societies dedicated ideologically and technologically to change. Sociologists meet equivalent problems in inter-national relations, central/local government, education, urbanization, race relations, sexual and marital behaviour, etc.

I have given these illustrations to show that health and medicine, and the institutional structures through which service is delivered, contain elements which are non-medical and which are the proper concern of sociologists. I shall develop these themes in separate chapters dealing with social structure, health beliefs, the profession of medicine, and the health system and shall indicate in concluding chapters some of the methodological approaches and problems of sociology. For non-sociologists, to whom this book is addressed, it may be helpful to say something about sociology, and especially medical sociology, and the possible contributions they might make to the understanding of health problems.

Many sciences have contributed to the development of medicine. Most sciences define the scope and content of their work by criteria intrinsic to their discipline and maintain an existence outside of, and independent from, medicine. They have shared in the development of medical science because the phenomena and processes defined by their discipline manifest themselves in the physiology and chemistry of the human body and the behaviour of human beings as well as in other parts of the natural world. They have also been drawn into the medical area because their knowledge and skills have relevance to medicine as an applied science. In principle sociology only differs from such sciences by its late arrival on the medical scene and by its intrinsic disciplinary content and methodologies. Sociology is about social inter-action, about the processes by which social relations are ordered and about the structures and institutions within which and by which they occur and are sustained. Since human objectives and situations differ widely, contradiction, disturbance, and conflict occur within and between parts of the social system, and the ways in which social order is both maintained and disrupted are an integral concern of sociologists. These interests can be, and are studied across the social 'system' in government, the economy, and social life. The sociology of health and of medicine is paralleled by other sociologies, of education, social welfare, marriage and the family, race-relations, deviance, and crime, etc. For most sociologists the ultimate objective is understanding (both looser and more comprehensive than explanation), but few would reject the possibility that their work might have some practical implications and many have chosen a particular field because it provides opportunities for applying sociological knowledge to current policy and substantive problems.

Medical sociologists are not entirely happy about the title of their specialty, because their concerns are with health and illness as much as with medicine and because the term medicine does not explicitly cover the range of healing and caring occupations and institutions with which they deal. A more precise description of their interests would specify health and illness, the health professions and their work, health services, health policy, and the health system, and it would be important to include on the one hand those aspects of social structure, social life, and beliefs which influence both health and medicine and, on the other, those contiguous service systems dealing with social welfare which maintain a fluid boundary-line with the health system. Such central sociological concepts as conflict, co-operation or the division of labour can only be partially explored within the confines of the health system itself.

Sociologists are aware that the processes by which knowledge is converted into action are themselves socially-influenced and might, at their most modest, merely hope that by widening and deepening the knowledge base and providing a new formulation of problems from their distinctive viewpoint, they might have an ultimate, if incalculable, impact upon decisions. More optimistically they might see their work having several kinds of practical relevance by:

1. Providing greater knowledge and understanding of those features of our social and economic system which promoted or inhibited the attainment and maintenance of health, or which produced illness and disease. This is neither epidemiology nor aetiology but the study of social processes which differentially lead some socially-defined groups to be exposed to known risks of disease, either through social beliefs or behaviour or the exigencies of their domestic and working lives. Direct implementation of such findings is likely to be more in the realm of social and health policy than of practising medicine. As a by-product such research may throw light on aetiological issues by suggestion or completing a chain of causation or making certain theories of exposure seem improbable. The work of George Brown (1978) on the role of life-events in the origins of clinical depression falls clearly into this aetiologically relevant category.

2. Documenting the health beliefs and health-related behaviour of social groups and the origins of specific systems of belief and behaviour in aspects of the social structure. Such knowledge is potentially relevant to social policy, health education and health-promotion, and to the initiation or re-structuring of services. If we are correct in thinking that the organization of services is

strongly influenced by the needs of service-providers, then systematic knowledge about potential clients' beliefs, behaviour, self-perceived needs and expectations provides corrective guidance to policy-makers, administrators, and service professionals.

3. Identifying and documenting trends in social behaviour likely to influence levels of health, types of illness, and the character, volume, and distribution of resources. Demography gives a numerical framework for questions about birth, marriage, death, and migration, but the interpretation of trends, their origins, consequences and subjective meanings, require other sociological research methods. Changes in sexual and marital behaviour, in the status, identity, and behaviour of women, and changes in drug use or drinking behaviour are relevant examples. They provide the background data for the planning and adaptation of services and for the revision of medical education and of doctor-patient relationships.

4. Examining the organizational dynamics of services and their relationship to the self-perceived needs of patients, their general objectives and the specific objectives of different types of service-provider. In effect this is the sociological evaluation of the structure and operation of services with emphasis placed not only upon outcome but upon the articulation of services and the concordance or discordance between the objectives of participants and between objectives and structures. It can be applied to simple units of study like a consultation, to a clinical service, to the co-ordination of medical and social services and to the development and implementation of policy. It has, therefore, a wide potential relevance.

5. Studying the development and formulation of policy, the assumptions and information upon which it is based, the process of decision-making and the implementation of policy, and the constraints and barriers to implementation. Again such studies of policies, systems, and action are conducted across a range of clinical fields and from the small-scale operation of a health centre to central government departments. They may have an equally wide range of relevance.

This is, of course, only one classification of research activity. It would have been differently structured by other sociologists and in practice any programme of research is likely to straddle these categories. The following chapters present some of the topics and the methodologies of medical sociology in more depth. In reading them it is important to keep in mind that sociologists are not doctors, that their central concern is the understanding of the processes, determinants, and consequences of social interaction and not the treatment of patients. Somewhere between the extremes of sociological theory and the laying-on of hands there is an area of mutually helpful overlap.

2

Social structure
and health

Since the days of the celebrated epidemiologists of the early and middle nineteenth century there has been no dearth of discoveries linking disease to environmental conditions and experience. From the overcrowding of poor populations in large insanitary cities, through the polluted atmosphere of industrial life and the dangers of heavy traffic to cigarette smoking and inadequate exercise, epidemiologists have demonstrated the effect of social and environmental experience on such diverse conditions as infectious diseases, the cancers, industrial and traffic accidents, chronic bronchitis, and heart disease. If we add differences in class and regional mortality revealed periodically by the Decennial Census, the total volume of known socially induced illness and premature death is formidable. Aetiological research tends to concentrate upon specific disease conditions. There are good reasons for such specificity. For technical reasons, research into specific conditions is most likely to reveal cause-and-effect relationships. And for therapeutic reasons physicians require illness to be broken down into separate, treatable entities. In any case, we have not yet developed satisfactory overall measures of illness and death, and the aggregation of conditions of differing aetiology might well, through cancelling-out effects, understate the true position. The net result is an insoluble jig-saw puzzle, in which the perceptible pieces receive more attention than the fragmented ungraspable whole. Specificity may assist diagnosis and treatment of the individual, but it hides the implications for political, economic, and social policy which might emerge from a more holistic presentation.

Sociologists attempt to go beyond the limitations imposed by a specific diseases approach to view causation at a different level,

11

and with different implications for the level of intervention required (Najman, 1980). Some sociologists are indeed interested in tracing the links between a health condition and particular facets of social life and individual experience—between coronary heart disease and the patterns of exercise and diet, between 'life-events' and depression, or between maternal deprivation and childhood handicap. Sociology in general, however, does not take disease as its starting point or as its central interest. Its primary concerns are social structure, social relationships, and social processes. Social structure refers to the major institutions of a society, the state, the economy, the family, the cultural, religious, scientific, medical, and educational systems, and the power relationships within and between them; the division of labour and the distribution of the social and economic product between significant groupings of the society distinguished by their age, sex, ethnicity, religion, education, and above all by their class position or their relationship to the means of production. These structural factors are seen as major determinants of individual and group behaviour. From this viewpoint, observed patterns of health and disease are seen as particular manifestations of the social structure, and medicine is regarded as a social institution reflecting the political, economic and social relationships of the society. Changes in the social and economic structure give rise to changes in health-related behaviour and health status and to changes in both the concepts and the organization of medicine. Associations between specific diseases and selected items of behaviour are pieces of empirical evidence about the social structure and the processes occurring within it, but they remain esoteric sociological knowledge until they are placed in the context of other observations and within an encompassing body of theory and knowledge about the working of social institutions. The differing objectives and perspectives of physicians and sociologists are a potent source of mutual misunderstanding; sociologists are apt to regard physicians (and particularly laboratory-based medical research workers) as a-theoretical empiricists and technicians whilst sociologists are regarded as grandiose theorists, prone to ideology and uninterested in practical therapeutic problems.

Some medical historians and epidemiologists provide a bridge between the disciplines. McKeown's work (1976) was sociologically exciting, not because of his contention that medicine's role in the reduction of mortality and morbidity had been exaggerated but because he used his professional knowledge to build up from specific diseases to a general picture of man, medicine, and society. His analysis showed the character of disease created by the social economic structure of nineteenth century Britain, the structural and associated behavioural changes which brought a reduction of mortality and the relative unimportance of medical knowledge and personal medical practice. He further demonstrated how the medical knowledge and practice developed out of nineteenth century medical problems was tangential to the new health problems created by societal change in the mid-twentieth century.

McKeown limits his prescriptions to suggesting an alternative, and more effective role for medicine in the prevention of abnormal birth, the protection of the well and the care of the sick, disabled, and dying. I would pick out another conclusion—that protection of the well by medical specialists can only be one part, and perhaps a minor part, of a general strategy which must entail political and economic action to rectify, at the structural level, the inequalities and inefficiencies which our present structure creates. This viewpoint has been forcibly expressed by Hart (1978):

Doctors are probably only too well aware that many of the most effective steps that could be taken to prevent ill-health in contemporary society would probably not involve medical expertise at all. Instead they would involve measures such as the following: Re-routing of heavy traffic away from the most densely populated residential areas, which also happen to be working-class neighbourhoods; free milk and high quality food at school; more aggressive legislation to prevent industrial accidents and diseases; a complete ban on smoking in public places; greater stability of employment and income in the economy; the removal of economic sanctions for sickness amongst manual workers and so on. Together such measures would represent an attack on the structure of inequality in Britain.

The implication is that, as a policy objective, the medical definition of health is inadequate. In accepted usage health is seen as the business of doctors and related professions. And in the prevailing organization of health services, that business is conducted almost entirely within hospitals, clinics, and general practitioner offices on a personal service basis. The nub of McKeown's argument, however, is that health and ill-health are created by social and economic conditions and associated behaviour which are outwith the professional competence and the accepted role of medicine. A DHSS memorandum (1976) attempted to widen the sphere of responsibility by suggesting that health is 'everybody's business' but its argument is most forceful in dealing with the individual's own responsibility for his personal health and is weakest in its statement about what central government and collective action can do.

Much of the responsibility for ensuring his own good health lies with the individual. We can all influence others by our own actions. In particular, parents can set their children a good example of healthy living. We can all help to influence the communities in which we live and work as much by our example as by our efforts.

In central government the Health Departments can set standards, spread ideas, finance health education, provide technical support and sponsor research. But prevention is also the concern directly or indirectly of other Departments [there follows a list of such Departments].

Making allowance for the fact that government departments often feel the need to express themselves in ambiguous generalizations this is hardly a prescription for dealing with class inequality in diet, housing, and education, with the industrial and urban environment or with the problems brought about by cigarettes and alcohol, all of which can only adequately be handled by collective political action.

In this chapter I wish to explore three aspects of social structure whose crude relationship to health and illness are already well documented. They are taken only as examples, my purpose being to discuss some of the ways in which they are seen by sociologists. I am particularly interested in how sociologists might get behind the bare fact of a relationship to describe the social processes which link structure with health and to demonstrate where epidemiology and vital statistics end and where sociology begins.

Social structure and health

Social class analysis is a long-established epidemiological tool for identifying the influence on death and disease of the socio-economic position and experience of individuals and of population groups. It is based on the recognition that occupation is a sensitive indicator, not only of working conditions but also of income, education, housing, diet, and a variety of social, economic and cultural characteristics which are often loosely described as 'life-style'. The pragmatic aggregation of occupations into social classes is usually intended to diminish the impact of the specific features of an occupation, such as environmental exposure at work, and to emphasize the more general component of life-style shared by different occupational groups. Since almost all adult men, and an increasing proportion of women, have paid employment, it is a convenient mechanism for subdividing and describing a total population, and since the boundaries between classes are not based upon a single over-riding criterion, the number of classes can be increased or decreased, concertina-wise, to suit the analytical problem and the exigencies of the data. In practice, in medical research it has become customary to divide the population into five Social Classes, each with its roman numeral and the Registrar-General provides a handbook which allows automatic allocation of a (precisely-worded) occupation to its appropriate class. The Registrar-General has repeatedly warned that between Censuses new occupations arise while old ones are re-assessed and re-classified and that, over time, occupations acquire a different significance. The persistence since 1921, however, of those five handy roman numerals creates the impression of stability and solidity, as though each class existed as something real and substantial rather than being an aggregative device used by research workers for analytical purposes.

The reification of Social Class causes many interpretative hazards. It tempts analysts into over-simplifications, and particularly into concluding that an abnormality is 'due to social class'. What is important, however, is not social class, but what lies behind the classification in terms of the social and biological

15

processes which link an occupational title and a disease. The environmental exposures and behavioural habits which distinguish Social Class I and Social Class III are different from those occurring between Classes III and V. No differences between groups in their illness are 'due to social class'—it is merely that social classification suggests the existence of socio-economic influences whose origins, nature, and mode of transmission need to be separated out and identified. For many medical scientists, however, class is an inconvenient contaminant, to be 'controlled out' in order that biological relationships can be more purely identified.

My main concern is with interpretations of class differences across time or between areas. Comparisons across time are usually intended to reveal whether a difference in mortality/morbidity has become greater or less, with the further intention of inferring whether socio-economic inequality has increased or decreased or whether health service treatment has become more or less equal. The important pre-condition of such a comparison is that each class should sample the same segment of the population on both occasions both numerically and sociologically. If like is not compared with like, then the resulting 'change' will be partially a function of the classification system rather than of social change.

Just as a class may change its significance over time, it is unlikely, given the geographical heterogeneity of our economy, that the same class title will contain comparable populations in widely differing industrial/geographical areas. Semi-skilled work may mean agricultural workers in one area and iron and steel workers in another, and it is unlikely that their levels of living and environmental exposures will possess the same resemblance as their Class title. (OPCS, 1978). The regional dissimilarity in Social Classes is least marked in Social Class I because professional workers not only have similar education, levels of living, and behavioural styles, but they also migrate more frequently between areas so that in many instances only a minority may work where they were reared. Workers at the semi-skilled and unskilled ends of the scale are more likely to reflect the economic and cultural state of their area of residence so that there may, certainly at the extremes, be little justification in thinking of Social Class V as sharing a common culture or experience.

Social structure and health

Richard Titmuss in the 1940s and Jerry Morris in the 1950s drew attention to the remarkable phenomenon that although neonatal and infant mortality rates had fallen heavily over the decades, they had fallen at the same rate in each social class (Titmuss, 1943; Morris and Heady, 1955). The gap between class rates was therefore as wide in 1951 as it was in 1911, 1921, and 1931. Yet major changes had occurred in our societies which might have been expected to reduce inequalities in health—particularly following full employment during and after the Second World War, and the introduction of the National Health Service in 1948. Various possibilities were raised. The concept of cultural lag was invoked to suggest the possibility that whilst structural changes had occurred, it took longer to change the living environment and the life-styles of individuals and social groups. Such arguments would also apply to the time-scale of changes in physique and general health. Additionally, there was good evidence to suggest that the middle-classes would be the first to take advantage of the benefits of a free health service, and thus temporarily widen the gap.

All these temporal arguments, perhaps plausible in the early 1950s, have much less validity today, a generation after the Second World War and the introduction of the National Health Service. Yet, as can be seen from Table 2.1., despite a heavy fall

TABLE 2.1. *Changes in still-birth, neonatal and post-neonatal death-rates by Social Class 1951–4 to 1974–7 (Scotland)*

Social Class	Still-birth rate	Neonatal death-rate	Post-neonatal death-rate
		1951–4	
I & II	21·0	15·8	5·8
III	24·8	20·9	11·9
IV & V	29·6	23·5	17·1
		1974–7	
I & II	7·9	8·3	3·1
III	10·2	11·0	4·5
IV & V	12·3	11·8	6·4
Rate in Social Class IV & V as a percentage of Class I & II.			
1951–4	141	149	295
1974–7	155	142	206

17

in death-rates, the relationship of still-birth rates and neonatal death-rates in Classes IV and V to those of Classes I and II is virtually unchanged (rates for separate classes were grouped to lessen the effect of classificatory changes over the period). Post-neonatal deaths, those most directly exposed to environmental influences, did begin to converge in the 1970s and it seems possible that at very low rates of death the environmental component will become increasingly dominated by congenital components not differentiated by class. Data on infant death for England and Wales up to the 1971 census period showed an undisturbed parallelism from 1911 to 1971. Classificatory changes over this long period may have affected particular class rates from time to time but could not have produced such parallelism.

One, very reasonable, reaction has been to question whether, after all, access to the benefits of medical care has been equally available to all social classes. There are good reasons for questioning whether free access to all, on a cafeteria basis, can itself produce equalization in the face of continuing class disparity in so many areas of social life, from income, housing and diet, to education, attitudes, and daily personal habits. Cognisant of the social aetiology of perinatal death, which stresses the previous long-term health and social history of the mother as a crucial component in her reproductive efficiency, others have questioned the predominantly medical/disease orientation of our services and have suggested that insufficient attention has been paid to public health and prevention (Chalmers, 1979; McKeown, 1976). Sociologists have generalized from similar data to question how far post-war equalization of living standards in the post-war welfare state has been more apparent than real. They accept the overall rise in living standards, but emphasize the persistence of relative inequality which parallels inequalities of reproductive mortality (Townsend, 1979; Westergaard and Resler, 1975).

In the 1950s I advanced an interpretation which attempted to combine a number of such factors by reference to the processes which led to social differentiation between occupational classes and the mechanisms which linked health to occupational position (Illsley, 1955, 1956a). At any point in time it is possible to account for particular disparities by invoking arguments relevant to that historical moment. When, however, relative disparity of almost the same degree persists across historical periods characterized by social and medical conditions so vastly different as 1911, 1931, 1951 and 1971, and substantial overall reductions in mortality have occurred over those years, a more fundamental, less particularistic explanation seems required. In view of the lack of change in relative class rates since my 1950s analysis, I have updated the material in order to explore further the reasons for continuing disparity.

Occupational classes are not solid, material, unchanging objects. They are human intellectual constructs formed by aggregating together occupational groups which are thought to have some degree of homogeneity. They increase and decrease over time as the economy and technology change, and they are subject to continuous reformation as individuals leave and die and as others are born and enter. We cannot have more people in an occupational class than the number of positions which the economy creates, but we can and do recruit more or less people into classes as the relevant occupations increase or decrease. A major factor determining the aggregated characteristics of a class in a mobile society (as opposed to castes in a static society) must be the selectivity of recruitment and exit. We know with some certainty the qualities necessary for death-free reproduction—they consist of good physical growth and general health, the diet, exercise, medical care, and freedom from noxious environmental exposure which promote physical growth in childhood and adolescence and sustain maternal health, allied to the knowledge, motivation and opportunity to plan reproduction and to make use of medical services for the detection and treatment of abnormal occurrences (Baird and Thomson, 1963). If one occupational class recruits a high proportion of such individuals whilst another recruits individuals of opposite characteristics and this occurs continuously over time, the maintenance of class differences is automatic. It will also be reinforced if conditions of life in the new class are equivalent to those which caused the transition into it. The process was described by an early sociologist as follows: 'physical superiority has been the condition which has favoured the social promotion of individuals and has facilitated their social climbing,

19

TABLE 2.2. *Social mobility and socio-medical characteristics. First pregnancies to married women Aberdeen City 1951–4*

Maternal characteristic	Class of upbringing	Inter-class movement			Class at marriage
	I & II (father)	left	entered	stayed	I & II (husband)
Percentage intelligence test grade above average	59	48	77	79	78
Percentage left school after minimum age	51	32	41	79	60
Percentage in professional, technical and clerical occupations	66	50	66	90	77
Percentage 5′ 4″ or more in height	41	32	42	50	46
Percentage physique and health good or very good	81	76	81	89	85
Rate of low birth-weight (per 100 births)	5·4	6·9	6·8	3·6	5·2
Rate of perinatal deaths (per 1000 births)	28	26	14	30	22
	IV & V				IV & V
Percentage intelligence grade above average	31	37	24	21	22
Percentage left school after minimum age	5	6	5	1	3
Percentage in professional, technical and clerical occupations	16	22	14	7	10
Percentage 5′ 4″ or more in height	23	24	20	21	21
Percentage physique and health good or very good	60	65	56	51	53
Rate of low birth-weight (per 100 births)	9·1	8·0	11·6	11	11·3
Rate of perinatal deaths (per 1000 births)	41	33	55	55	55

while physical inferiority has facilitated the "social sinking" of individuals and their location in the lower social strata' (Sorokin 1959).

This thesis was based upon data collected in 1951–4 for women having a first pregnancy in Aberdeen and for a sub-sample on whom more varied and intensive data were obtained. The results are summarized in Table 2.2.

Taking Social Classes I and II the data show that those brought up in these classes who married into Classes IV and V, had lower scores on I.Q. tests, left school earlier, and entered less prestigious occupations. They were shorter in stature, had poorer physique, and had a higher perinatal death rate in their first pregnancies. Other data not presented here but given in the original thesis show that their dietary intake was lower in protein, calcium, and vitamins A, B, and C. In respect of low birth weight the change was not selective, but on a larger population based on all pregnancy numbers rather than first pregnancies alone, the exchange was clearly and positively selective on both low birth weight and perinatal death.

Table 2.2. also gives similar data for Social Classes IV and V. The position is reversed in that entrants have less favourable characteristics than those marrying out of Classes IV and V into higher classes.

The 1956 analysis also showed that this selective exchange occurred equally for that sizeable group who during pregnancy were still, in the housing conditions of the 1950s, living in their parental homes and also for those, who having conceived pre-nuptially, had only been exposed to their husband's class environment for a few months. This seemed to rule out the possibility that reproductive mobidity and mortality was due to post-marital social, economic, and environmental conditions. Indeed taking the pre-pregnancy indicators, e.g. height and education, the selective exchange was equally marked in the class mobility occurring before marriage between the social class of the woman's father and her own pre-marital occupation.

The picture emerges of social classes of upbringing being relatively heterogeneous in terms of the actual experience of children within each class. Variations in diet and the living standards which predispose to optimal growth and development are positively correlated with factors such as education and IQ (the latter being taken not as a genetic indicator but as a reflection of environmental stimulation) which predispose to occupational attainment and, in turn, through assortive mating to upward mobility on marriage. As a result, class differences, both social and biological, which occur when persons are classified by their class of up-bringing, are sharpened when they are re-classified by class at marriage. The processes of social mobility thus possess an in-built differentiating quality, which continues year by year with each new cohort and produces a pressure towards disparity. This could, of course, be overcome if mobility were reduced, if it became more random, or if the link between social/educational and biological/health development were weakened.

Repetition of the identical analysis for the 1970s is not possible because the 1950s data were derived from specially-mounted studies. A few crucial indicators are, however, available from the routine statistics of the Aberdeen Maternity and Neo-Natal Data Bank and they are shown in Table 2.3. The same processes are clearly operative 20 years later. We are therefore dealing, as postulated above, with a continuous process producing a constant

TABLE 2.3. *Social mobility and socio-medical characteristics. First pregnancies to married women Aberdeen District* 1969–75*

Maternal characteristic	Class of upbringing I & II (father)	Inter-class movement left	entered	stayed	Class at marriage I & II (husband)
Percentage in professional technical and clerical occupations	71	62	74	81	77
Percentage 5′ 4″ or more in height	45	41	41	50	45
Rate of low birth-weight	6·6	7·8	4·7	5·1	4·9
Rate of perinatal death	20	22	9	18	12
	IV & V				IV & V
Percentage in professional, technical and clerical occupations	40	47	40	24	32
Percentage 5′ 4″ or more in height	29	32	32	24	28
Rate of low birth-weight	6·7	5·5	10·3	9·3	9·8
Rate of perinatal death	15	12	26	19	24

* Boundary changes brought in a large suburban area making the Aberdeen City of 1951–4 not strictly comparable with the Aberdeen District of 1969–75.

tendency to widen class differences. Just as the 1911–51 differences survived great historical changes, so the 1951–75 differences persist through the remarkable changes in reproductive behaviour accompanying birth control, abortion, and sterilization.

Both in the 1950s and the 1970s there were, of course, differences between classes in their use and experience of medical care which would be likely to accentuate disparity in mortality and morbidity. Classes still differ in their use of antenatal services and in health related behaviour such as dietary intake and smoking during pregnancy. However, the known and accepted aetiology of perinatal death, and particularly of still-births, suggests the operation of long-term influences, related to physical growth and development, rather than short-run within-pregnancy factors. Class differences in low birth weight have also continued unchanged over these years with no decrease in any class and there seems little likelihood that medical intervention has much, if any, influence on the distribution of low birth weight.

One other major feature of class formation must be mentioned. Whilst relative class mortality rates remain unchanged, the size of classes has changed as a result of occupational shifts in the economy and of changes in the classification of occupations. There have also been changes in fertility, the largest falls being in the manual working-classes. Out of all live births in England and Wales only 12 per cent were to Class I and II mothers in 1931 compared with 16 per cent in 1951 and 22 per cent in 1970–2. The largest decrease in size occurred in Social Class V which fell from 20 per cent of live births in 1931 to 6 per cent in 1970–2. The largest increases in births therefore took place in the classes with the lowest death rates and the largest decreases in the classes with exceptionally high rates. Reduction in class mortality has therefore manifested itself in two ways. First, death rates have fallen equally in all classes. Second, the highest class death rates now apply to a smaller segment of the population. As a result, Social Class V contributed only 11 per cent of all deaths of legitimate infants in 1970–2 compared with 25 per cent in 1931. This is one instance where the use of death rates can be misleading unless accompanied by consideration of the number of deaths to which they apply.

It is also important to consider carefully the questions under-lying the measures we use. In the consideration of class death rates over time there are at least three separate questions which occasionally become entangled. The first asks, what proportion of all deaths derive from particular classes? We have already seen that Social Class V now contributes only 11 per cent of legitimate infant deaths. Whilst this is disproportionately high compared with the number of births, the policy implication is that any fur-ther major reduction in reproductive mortality must now come from higher classes and particularly from the manual working Classes III and IV which between them contribute 63 per cent of all deaths. The second question, of a more political and sociologi-cal kind, asks about the range of equality and inequality in our society at different points in time; health and disease as proxy indicators of the total range of inequality and of the relationships between strata. Judged by class death rates the answer must be that relative inequality has not changed greatly over many decades. The conclusion however would require heavy qualifi-cation. Death rates may only imperfectly reflect social and econ-omic inequality, which for its more accurate and comprehensive measurement requires evidence drawn from a multitude of indi-cators each appropriate to a particular aspect of social life (see Townsend, 1979). Moreover the method of classification de-veloped by the Registrar-General and applied to occupational mortality has serious deficiencies for comparisons over time. Ideally we need methods of classification which would allow us to rank the population according to a measure of class or of in-equality and to subdivide it so that, at each point in time we would be comparing segments of the population equivalent in ranking and in size. It is virtually impossible to interpret the meaning of a comparison over time between two classes of which one has doubled and the other halved as a proportion of the total popu-lation. Social Classes I and II are no longer the exclusive elites of the inter-war years and Class V has become a selected small minority. Any approach to issues of inequality in health using crude general indicators, without the detailed data required for their interpretation, is inadequate. The third question asks, do children brought up in different classes reflect their class upbring-

24

ing in later adult health? This is not so much an issue of equality per se but of equality of opportunity equivalent to parallel questions concerning educational opportunity. I have attempted to disentangle the two latter questions in a re-presentation of the mobility data concerning married Aberdeen primiparae in 1951–4 and 1969–75. For simplicity of presentation I am assuming only two Classes, I and II combined and IV and V combined, but theoretically the model could apply to any number of classes and similar findings did result from a more complex analysis of the Aberdeen data using three classes. Figure 2.1. shows the periantal death rates of

1951–4. Aberdeen primiparae classified by their father's social class

1951–4. Aberdeen primiparae classified by their husband's social class

1969–75. Aberdeen primiparae classified by their father's social class

1969–75. Aberdeen primiparae classified by their husband's social class.

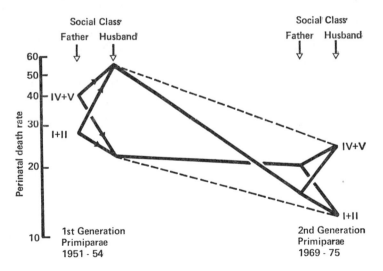

FIGURE 2.1. Maintenance of class differentials in perinatal death rates by selective exchange between classes.

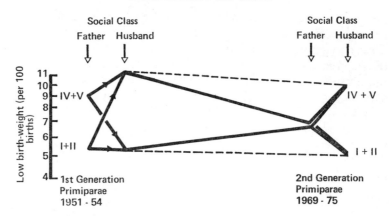

FIGURE 2.2. Maintenance of class differentials in low birth-weight rates by selective exchange between classes.

The outer parallel (broken) lines are the equivalent of those death rates derived from decennial supplements, being based at each point on the husband's social class. The lines at each end represent the inter-class exchange when women are re-classified from their class of upbringing to their class at marriage; the inner set of lines represent the death rates of women of an earlier generation classified by their marital class, and the death rates of a subsequent generation classified by their class of upbringing. Whilst these inner lines do not link actual mothers and daughters, they can be interpreted as such, because the second generation are the daughters of mothers of the same class separated by 15–24 years. The outer lines answer the question as to how far classes have remained apart; the inner lines answer the question about the effect of being brought up in a particular class. The outer lines remain apart, the inner lines converge. Figure 2.2. applies the same presentational analysis to low birth weight. Because the 'daughters' are only daughters of a class rather than true daughters, because in- and out-migration has occurred over the generation and because city boundaries have changed, the presentation is best regarded as a model based on best approximations.

It serves, however, the purpose of disentangling two questions and of illustrating a process which underlies and sustains the class structure. It also draws our attention to the empirical question which most requires elucidation, namely, *within each class*, what are the actual experiences of upbringing which, in aggregate, lead simultaneously to upward mobility and a good health status or to downward mobility and a poor health status? It further demonstrates the crudeness of occupational class as a predictor of future social status and health. Occupational classes are shown to be heterogeneous and not an adequate substitute for detailed knowledge of everyday life in those classes. Without the detailed case-by-case knowledge of actual experience of income and expenditure, of diet and living conditions, of intellectual stimulation and social expectations, of educational experience and social relationships, we cannot answer important questions. What are the respective influences of a cultural class milieu and of direct parental influences, of income and material living conditions and of social and economic values? At what stages can differentiation be identified? Does the process apply equally to all children in a family? How far is family size involved? Can education be seen to have a distinct impact contrary to prevailing sub-cultural or parental influences?

The interpretation of class differences is probably at its simplest at this stage of the life-cycle. In later life new influences will have been superimposed upon the effects of upbringing stemming from work and careers, marriage and family life, migration or residential change, accidents, chronic illnesses, and misfortunes. Intra-generational class movement will have caused further re-formation of classes.

Most sociological studies of social mobility have been concerned with the structure of classes and the relationship between classes and have collected their data retrospectively. Few have been concerned with the personal characteristics of the socially mobile and since data have usually been collected retrospectively do not provide direct data on social experience. The 1948 and 1958 samples initiated by James Douglas and by Neville Butler and now being followed longitudinally by the Medical Research Council and by the National Children's Bureau stop short of observational data but nevertheless yield useful material. If we are to take social class, its meanings and its effects on health further, such national studies must be supplemented, not once but periodically over the years, by small scale detailed studies in a variety of communities, and followed up long enough to see effects materialize in health behaviour and health status.

FAMILY, ABORTION, AND ILLEGITIMACY

Demographers, epidemiologists, and obstetricians, in research on reproductive patterns, tend to use a number of descriptive categories, such as social class, age and parity, marital status and family size, as broad parameters, making comparisons between these categories or studying trends within them. Past research has demonstrated that the social, biological, or interacting social and biological influences represented by these categories are so powerful that, unless they are considered separately, their effect on mortality and morbidity will obscure other features being studied. It is one method of 'making allowance for' or 'controlling out' variables extraneous to the problem being studied. It is a useful analytical device. It can also be misleading if the use of such categories is not accompanied by an informed and data-based understanding of the categories themselves. In the previous section I dealt with one of these categories, social class, and showed that class acquired its meaning through its relationship to a changing social structure and through a complicated process of selective interchange. Misleading results emerged through treating class as a variable or a static entity unvarying in time and space. In this section I shall examine, from a similar viewpoint some of the other categories (or stereotypes) frequently used in demographic analysis.

Throughout reproductive statistics legitimate and illegitimate births are presented separately. There is one simple administrative rationale for such a procedure; when births to a woman are classified according to the occupation of her husband, births to an unmarried woman or to a married woman whose husband does not register the child as his own, present a classificatory problem. There are, however, other reasons some of a historical or legal nature, some relating to risks attaching to illegitimate pregnancy, and particularly the perinatal and postnatal mortality of illegitimate infants. The infant mortality rate of illegitimate infants in the UK has been between 50–100 per cent higher than that of legitimate infants in the last few decades and such sharp differences are familiar, country by country, in the Western industrial world back into the nineteenth century. The latest available figures for Scotland (1977) show that the still-birth neonatal and post-neonatal death rates of illegitimate births are 67, 75, and 91 per cent respectively higher than the equivalent rates for legitimate births. There are therefore good epidemiological reasons for continuing to treat illegitimacy as a separate statistical category. There are, however, equally good reasons for thinking that the social and biological significance of illegitimate status may have undergone many changes not reflected in demographic trends but having implications for the family as a social institution and for maternal and child health services.

Illegitimacy is a legal status and its incidence and the internal composition of the category can be shifted by legal changes—as indeed occurred in the 1970s through changes in the divorce laws and rules relating to registration. More important is that illegitimate birth is the end point of a chain of social action and social and medical decision-making. As Macintyre (1977) shows in her study of single pregnant girls, the chain begins with the 'decision' to have intercourse, and to use or not to use effective contraception, and proceeds through the successive stages of the recognition of pregnancy, the willingness or ability of both partners to marry, and the decision (involving partners, parents, general practitioners, and gynaecologists) to continue or to terminate the pregnancy and to keep or place the child for adoption. The chain of events is affected by cultural sanctions on extra-marital intercourse, the availability and use of contraceptive techniques, legislation concerning both divorce and abortion, the attitudes and practice of general practitioners and gynaecologists, and the perceptions of partners and of advisers about the social costs of marriage as opposed to either abortion or illegitimate maternity. The social acceptability and the availability of these options and the legislative, medical, and cultural contingencies affecting them have changed over the last century and most dramatically over the last few decades (Illsley and Hall, 1976; Illsley and Taylor, 1974). Illegitimacy, in its social meaning, can hardly be regarded as an invariant phenomenon, but rather as a common legal status obscuring its internal composition and its external social significance.

Illegitimacy ratios (illegitimate births as a percentage of all births) fell throughout the late nineteenth century and the early decades of this century in Scotland from their highest point of 10·3 per cent in 1866, with major interruptions in the two World Wars, until they reached their lowest recorded level at 4·1 per cent in 1957. They then began a sharp rise reaching 9·8 per cent in 1978. The rates in England and Wales, historically lower than those of Scotland, reached their low point in 1953 several years earlier than those in Scotland and then began an almost continuous rise reaching 10 per cent in 1978.

The geographical and temporal phasing of the upturn of rates in the UK since the Second World War has interesting aetiological implications. The first signs of an upturn occurred in London in 1954 and this was quickly followed by rises in the large conurbations whilst rural rates were still falling. Whereas their rates were not dissimilar at the beginning of the period by the 1970s conurbation rates were double those of rural areas. Whilst the rise started later in Scotland its geographical spread was similar and again in the late 1970s the conurbation rate was double that of the rural areas.

An equally important change occurred in maternal age. In 1955, 16 per cent of Scottish illegitimate births were to women aged 19 or less and 31 per cent to women of 30 or more. By 1975 this had changed to 36·4 and 13·0. Whilst women having legitimate births were also younger the change was much less marked, only 10 per cent being 19 or less at the later date.

For other data on illegitimate pregnancy it is necessary, in the absence of national statistics, to rely on data for Aberdeen City and District collected continuously since 1951. The trend in rates and in maternal age mirrors the national picture but it becomes clear from the Aberdeen data that a marked shift in parity has occurred. Whereas in 1955 37 per cent of both legitimate and illegitimate births were to primiparae, in 1975 42 per cent of legitimate births were to primiparae compared with 70 per cent for illegitimate births. The marital status of mothers having illegitimate births also changed during the period. Early data for Aberdeen City are available from a specially conducted study by Dr Barbara Thompson (1956) for the years 1949–52. Comparison with a later study (Illsley and Gill, 1968) suggests that the proportion of illegitimate births to married women fell from 37 per cent in 1949–52 to 18 per cent in 1966.

These findings are, however, only numerical indicators, along a few dimensions, of the social movements occurring over the period. Further clarification can be obtained by studying some components in the chain of events linking extra-marital intercourse to illegitimate birth. Given the paucity of reliable data, quantified estimates of the frequency of extra-marital intercourse and of associated contraceptive use carry little credibility, although there is little doubt that extra-marital intercourse has increased substantially, particularly among teenagers and that the circumstances of extra-marital relationships and of young single persons promote non-use or irregular use of effective contraceptive techniques (Illsley and Taylor, 1974). Data are available however on other links of the chain, some of which are presented in Table 2.3.

Taking 1955 as the baseline I have calculated at 5 year intervals the index numbers for major constituents of reproduction. After a rise into the early 1960s the number of legitimate births fell rapidly and particularly the number of third and subsequent births indicating, not only the preference for one- and two-child families, but also the impact of more widespread and effective contraception following the introduction of the pill around 1964. The frequency of conception before marriage, but followed by marriage, continued to rise until 1970. This reflected increased pre-marital sexual activity, particularly among teenagers at a time when reliable contraceptives were not readily available to young unmarried women and when habits of contraceptive use in unmarried couples had not become established (Illsley and Taylor, 1974). Pre-maritally conceived births decreased rapidly in the 1970s following the introduction of legalized abortion. This provided an alternative to the two previously available options of marriage or of illegitimate maternity. Throughout the

TABLE 2.3. *Index numbers of changing reproductive trends in Scotland (1955=100)*

Legitimate live births						
1st	100	102	98	93	81	74
2nd	100	109	104	95	84	81
3+	100	112	114	81	43	37
Legitimate pre-maritally						
conceived 1st births	100	108	125	143	101	83
Illegitimate live births	100	110	147	168	158	150
Abortions to married women				100	114	107
Abortions to single						
widowed/separated and						
divorced women				100	166	173

period, and not reversed (though possibly limited) by the introduction of the pill and of legal abortion, the illegitimacy ratio continued to rise.

These changes in the response to pre-maritally-conceived pregnancy were gradual, most pronounced in the early stages among the professional groups, permeating less skilled groups at a slower pace. This is shown by data on first pregnancies to women single at conception assembled by Dr Barbara Thompson (Thompson and Aitken-Swan, 1973) and recently updated by her (Fig. 2.3.). Professional women, students, and nurses earliest and increasingly took the option of termination and by 1974–7 nearly 80 per cent of pre-maritally conceived first pregnancies in this group were terminated. Correspondingly the proportion who married whilst pregnant decreased at almost the same rate. The proportion giving birth to an illegitimate child hardly varied across these fifteen years. Among clerical workers, shop assistants and skilled manual workers the option of termination built up more slowly and by 1974–7 occurred in just less than 50 per cent of cases. Among unskilled workers termination came still later, and by 1974–7 occurred in approximately three out of ten pregnancies. In all groups the compensating fall occurred in marriage during pregnancy whilst the proportion having an illegitimate child varied only slightly over the whole period. Year-by-year analysis suggests that in the professional group the proportion having an illegitimate child may be falling and that in the other groups the

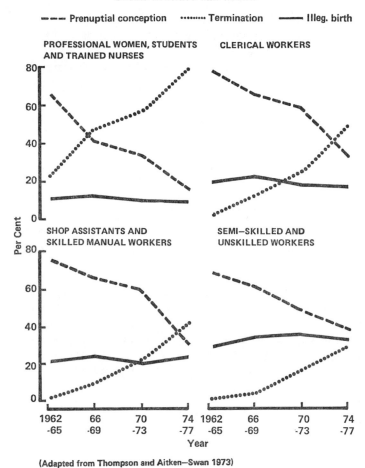

(Adapted from Thompson and Aitken—Swan 1973)

FIGURE 2.3. Outcome of first pregnancies to women single at conception by occupational group (Aberdeen City 1962–77).

trends shown in Fig. 2.3. are continuing. A number of points emerge from this historical review of options following pre-marital conception.

1. That throughout the period 1962–78 covered by these data there was continuous change occurring in the responses to pre-maritally conceived pregnancy, with lower occupational groups

successively taking up the pattern of responses adopted earlier by higher occupational groups. It seems likely that the full impact of change has yet to be seen.

2. That initial reaction has been an increase in termination accompanied by a corresponding fall in the number of women who regularize pregnancy by marriage. The availability of termination has thus provided the opportunity to avoid premature marriage and parenthood.

3. That the proportion of first pregnancies conceived outside marriage which result in illegitimate births has been relatively constant over the period, a decrease appearing only late in the period and still mainly confined to the upper social groups.

This piecing-together of demographic data from disparate sources provides a bare statistical framework. It leaves many unanswered questions about which we can only make inferences from inadequate evidence. At the societal level, we are still unclear about the structural origins of such remarkable changes in sexual mores, courtship patterns, and reproductive behaviour in teenagers and young persons. Most major changes in social behaviour affecting large sections of society do have their origins in economic and technological developments but they can only be traced by understanding their subjective meaning to individuals whose separate actions, when aggregated, constitute a social movement. Unfortunately sociologists were rather rare in the 1950s and 1960s and family sociology had a low status in the profession at that time so that the basic observations on which sound theory could be built were never made. Similarly we can make inferences about the differential pace at which social groups availed themselves of legalized abortion, based on general theories of the dissemination of ideas and behaviour from high status to low status groups. But there is some evidence to suggest (Aitken-Swan, 1973 and 1977; Macintyre, 1977) that demand was filtered selectively by general practitioners and consultants and that the case for abortion from upper and lower social groups was differently presented and differently perceived by decision-makers. Even more difficult to interpret is the continuing rise of illegitimacy ratios in the face of more freely-available and effective contraceptives and of relatively free access to abortion in areas such as Aberdeen.

34

Does the invariant proportion of pre-maritally conceived pregnancies which end in illegitimate birth within each class signify technical barriers to marriage, ethical objections to abortion, decisions made too late in pregnancy to permit abortion, or has illegitimate birth and unmarried motherhood acquired a different cultural meaning? One theory would suggest that the very high frequency of illegitimate birth (now approximately 15 per cent of first births to single women in urban Scotland) is evidence either that the stigma of illegitimacy has already been reduced or that it cannot be maintained. A related theory suggests that it signifies a different approach to marriage—a trial period of cohabitation and parenthood which will later be legalized by marriage, a theory given credence by the fact that the illegitimacy ratio of second and subsequent births appears, on the basis of Aberdeen data, to have remained over almost 20 years at a low level of 4–5 per cent. Reports from Sweden and Denmark (Dahlström and Liljeström, 1980) suggest that a majority of couples begin cohabitation without marrying and that their relationship is not essentially different from that of married couples. This possibility however does not fit some aspects of British experience and particularly the fact that, as the illegitimacy ratio has increased the relative disadvantages of illegitimate birth compared with legitimate birth in terms of still-births and infant deaths have worsened, from being 40 per cent higher in 1956 to 70 per cent higher in 1977 (Registrar-General Scotland, 1977). Given these uncertainties there is a very large gap in our knowledge of the subsequent health and welfare of both the parents and surviving children.

This extended example is intended to illustrate the complex behaviour lying behind demographic statistics, the processes which give rise to statistics, and the changing composition and social meaning of commonly used categories. Similar illustrations could be drawn out of other data relating to family formation and reproduction—the rise in divorces and re-marriage, the growth of the two-child family, the increasing use of female sterilization and of vasectomy, all of which have far-reaching implications for the fundamental social institutions of marriage and the family. The so-called 'hard data' of vital statistics are invaluable but their interpretation is uncertain without more

35

detailed knowledge and direct observations which allow us to explore the subjective meanings of behaviour and thus to substitute evidence for inference in our search for explanation.

In an attempt to evaluate the effectiveness of health services reference is frequently made to the international league tables of mortality (see, for example, Wynn and Wynn (1979) on maternal and child health services and the prevention of handicap). The underlying assumption often employed is that, if comparisons are restricted to developed industrial countries and particularly those of Northern Europe, at least a major part of the inter-country differences reflects the performance of our health system. When UK death rates are higher than those of 'comparable' countries, such comparisons provide a rhetoric for demanding increased resources for a particular service. Much concern has been expressed recently, for example, about the relatively slow decline in perinatal and infant mortality with the result that UK rates, which ranked well in the 1950s, and early sixties, have been overtaken by many of our industrial neighbours. International comparisons backed up by detailed analysis of the operation of services, identifying specific differences in death or illness and relating them to equally specific differences in service provision and organization, could certainly be revealing. General comparisons, however, present massive problems of interpretation. The underlying assumption of rough socio-economic equivalence does not withstand examination. Gross domestic product per head varies widely across developed societies and correlates well with perinatal mortality rates (Chamberlain, 1979). Trends and rankings in death rates over post-war years between the UK and other developed societies also correlate with changes in gross domestic product. Great Britain's fall in the league tables thus parallels its relatively slow rate of economic growth. Given the long-demonstrated relationship between infant mortality and income, perhaps the major lesson to be learnt from such general international comparisons is that health services which intervene at the point of illness cannot counteract the continuous impact of relatively low living standards. This point is emphasized by the very high correlations between infant mortality and other causes of death in adults. Countries, regions, and social classes with high or low death rates from infant mortality have corresponding rates for respiratory disease, heart disease, cerebrovascular disease, and the environmental cancers (Wynn and Wynn, 1979). The implications do not point to the reform of a particular clinical service but to measures for improving the basic health of the total population through higher living standards.

Similar conclusions must be drawn from a review of regional death rates within the UK. Four relevant points emerge:

1. That ranking of regional death rates for infant mortality and, for males aged 15–64 is almost identical.

2. That the variation between regions is least in Social Class I and increases with each step down the class range.

3. That both sets of differences have persisted over the last four censuses from 1931–71. Standard regions used for Census purposes have changed so that it is impossible to compare all regions across time. For five English regions with unchanged boundaries the rankings vary only slightly from decade to decade and the greater regional variability of the lower social classes persists throughout. There is however, a slight tendency for inter-regional variation to be reduced over time.

4. That standardization for social class reduces the inter-regional differences and produces marginally different rankings but neither eliminates the variations nor produces substantially different rankings. This latter point is hardly surprising in that occupational class distributions only represent one of the many social, economic and environmental differences existing between regions.

In the analysis of social class differences over time described earlier it emerged that systematic inter-change between classes through social mobility operated constantly to keep the class gap open. Migration does occur between regions, and it is known that such migration is selective, in that migrants out of a geographical area tend to have characteristics more favourable to health than those who remain. So also do those who migrate inwards to replace them. The process is highly complex, but allowing for the cancelling out effects of out-migrants and in-migrants and the lesser amount of geographical than social class mobility, the net inter-change is unlikely itself to maintain inter-regional differences or even to affect them significantly. Nor does the geographical variation in medical resources fit the variation in death rates (Coates and Rawstron, 1971). Some of the regions obtain low rates with relatively limited medical manpower and facilities and some of the regions with high rates have the largest input of resources per head. A few specific variations in health statistics can be explained on the basis of variations in health service policy—for example, the high Scottish rates of admission and stay in mental hospitals are probably attributable to conscious policies of hospitalization. Variations in other conditions of known aetiology, like cancer of the lung, are almost certainly due to differential patterns of behaviour. Regional differences in mortality however are long-standing, outlasting changes in health service policy and organization, prevailing across temporary behavioural patterns, and spreading over a wide range of diseases.

It is indeed the inclusiveness of these disease patterns which makes the search for specific causes of specific diseases so difficult and potentially misleading. Using 1970-2 data on socio-economic groups in England and Wales the Wynns (1979) demonstrated very high correlations between infant mortality and deaths from respiratory disease, diabetes, diseases of the circulatory system, ischaemic heart disease, cervical cancer, stomach cancer, etc. in married women. West (1977) studying ischaemic heart disease in regions and administrative areas of England and Wales tested and confirmed the hypothesis that the geographical pattern of IHD deaths corresponded so closely with the pattern of deaths from all causes that the existence of high IHD deaths in certain areas merely reflected a general tendency to early death in those areas compared with areas of low IHD mortality. When, instead of using standardized mortality ratios he employed proportional mortality ratios, which make allowance for variations in general death rates, he found a geographical pattern of excess deaths specifically due to ischaemic heart disease very different from the general patterns. My own analysis of regional IHD rates within Scotland produced similar results. West concluded:

38

The significant geographical differences within England and Wales are differences in *mortality* [my emphasis] and they are largely differences in age at death, irrespective of cause of death. The public health measures should not be directed towards eradicating 'an IHD specific toxin' in the England and Wales environment, since mortality from other causes demonstrates similar associations with socio-environmental variables, but should be directed towards alleviating early death from all causes (including IHD) by modifying the environmental microclimate and improving socio-economic circumstances.

Modification of the environmental micro-climate and improvement of economic circumstances is a tall order. Regional economic policy has been notionally committed to the redistribution of employment away from the affluent South and Midlands to depressed areas since the Barlow Commission report of 1940. Like the decentralization of the Civil Service it is always about to happen. The political and economic forces ranged against such a policy have so far proved insuperable. In a concern for the health of the nation it is easier (but not all that easy) to redistribute medical resources in order to deal more effectively with the results of continuing regional inequality.

West's prescription is demanding for other reasons. In what way should the environmental micro-climate be modified? And in considering the multitude of socio-economic circumstances to be improved, which should receive priority? It is at this point that our knowledge becomes extremely ragged. Some would argue, with much justification, that full employment and industrial redistribution would be enough to trigger the social, educational, dietary, and other behavioural changes which occurred spontaneously over many years in the South of England and in such countries as Sweden and the Netherlands. On grounds of morality, and in the absence of firm knowledge about social development in advanced societies, it is an attractive proposition —and such a levelling-up of living standards is a necessary, if not a sufficient objective. It is also a long process, beset by all the economic hazards and lack of political will which have prevented its earlier realization. As a sociological and political version of monetarism it could equally bring short-term deterioration in health-related behaviour.

The problem about an informed, engineered approach (if politically possible) is that we lack the basic knowledge of social

39

structure and of its implications for behaviour and behavioural change. I shall deal in a later section with current, conventional techniques of health education and disease prevention. For the moment I am concerned with another and more fundamental set of questions about the socio-economic structure (including but not confined to the three major topics of class, family, and region discussed in this chapter), its relationship to behaviour and the implications for health. The unanswered questions, both relevant to the problem, and of interest to the sociologist, are essentially ones of linkages between structure, position in structure, values and attitudes, health-related behaviour, and health status. Much research, from a proper concern to reach practical results quickly, has studied the linkages between a particular aspect of health or disease and one of these components of a continuously linked process. Some of the preceding examples of the relationship between infant mortality and social class, ischaemic heart disease and region, typify a common epidemiological approach. Nobody imagines that class or region, which are intellectual constructs, have a direct impact on infant mortality or ischaemic heart disease. They merely place an individual in a broad structural position and leave open for further study or inference the chain of interaction from structure, through life experience, health beliefs, and health-related behaviour to health outcomes. Some parts of the chain have received a lot of research attention. Political sociologists have studied intensively for many years and across countries and continents the relationship between political structure and the economic or the educational system, and other sociologists have looked, for example, at religious organization and family structure, or economic development and environmental change. Similarly there has been much research within other columns of Table 2.4, of the relationship between work, income, and expenditure, between knowledge, attitudes, and planning, between diet, drinking, smoking, and exercise or between the incidence of different diseases. There has also been research between the contiguous columns of Table 2.4, e.g. between eating, drinking, smoking, and disease. Given the infinite permutations of the pathways from social structure to health outcomes, for the variety of age, sex, and social groups,

TABLE 2.4. *From social structure to health outcomes*

Aspects of social structure	Everyday life experience of individuals	Health beliefs and orientations to health	Health-related behaviour	Health outcomes
Political	Income	Concepts of health	Eating	Growth
Economic	Expenditure	Health as a value	Drinking	Physique
Cultural	Work	Knowledge about health	Smoking	Illness
Medical	Education	Planning	Exercise	Disease
Religious	Family life	Risk-taking	Exposure	Stress
Familial	Social relationships	Prevention	Service-use	Handicap
Environ-mental	Physical and cultural milieu		Family planning	Well-being
			Child-rearing	

and a multiplicity of health conditions, the relative paucity of research across the spectrum is understandable. The goal, however, must surely be to understand the influence of structural influences across the columns as they impinge on the life-cycles of individuals. Perhaps most (and the most fruitful) research has been completed on the link between structural variables relating to population change where the combined efforts of demographers, anthropologists, sociologists, epidemiologists, and obstetricians have explored the linkage across many countries and social groups between economic development, religious and cultural beliefs, sexual activity, family formation, and reproductive outcomes. The importance of population size to economic activity, and to political power has stimulated some governments to invest in population research, the topic has been central to several academic disciplines, and the concentrated time-period of pregnancy has simplified both documentation and analysis. A new sub-speciality of the social sciences with the opaque title of 'population socialization' has recently emerged with linkages between structure, individual behaviour, and outcomes as its principal focus. Even in this well-researched field, however, subjective meanings are largely derived by inferences from behaviour.

In an excellent and comprehensive review of existing knowledge about transmitted inequalities in health Blaxter (1980) examined 'the relationship between genetic inheritance and inborn health, between maternal characteristics and infant health, between infant health and childhood health and (with less certainty of any answer) between childhood health and adult health'. In so doing she also attempted where possible to elucidate the interactions between structure, characteristics, behaviour, and health. She drew on many types of data—continuing large-scale descriptive statistics and particularly those of the Registrars-General and the Government Statistical Service; cross-sectional data relating to a cohort of the population studied at one point in time (e.g. the British Perinatal Mortality Survey); longitudinal data on a cohort followed over time, e.g. the National Survey of Health and Development; life-cycle studies (which were few and limited); focused explanatory studies using a limited number of variables; and ethnographic, descriptive and case-history studies designed to illustrate processes or explore the subjective meanings of events. Each had its major limitations for the particular purpose of tracing relationships. Whilst Blaxter's review uncovers many revealing associations, even her dexterous manipulation of sources frequently stops short of revealing causal relationships and linkages across the process of social-biological interaction, the data being too fragmented. The national statistics from the Registrars-General and the Office of Population Censuses and Surveys, of consistent high quality over many decades, deal with groups and aggregates (class, occupation, region, sex, and age) in which each group is large and heterogeneous in terms of the other variables; they are therefore of limited value in charting the pathways of individuals. Focused studies, often confined to the interests and concepts of a particular discipline, are difficult to relate back to population processes and may indeed be designed to control-out their influence. Particularly interested in inter-generational transmission Blaxter identifies life-long health 'career' studies as the present greatest need and specifically

documentation and analysis of the linkages at different points of the lifetimes of different groups of people: what are the relationships of different health patterns and different occupational career patterns? in what ways is health associated with upward or downward mobility? how easily can chronic adult ill-health be predicted in childhood? Viewed in their entirety, these are difficult questions, but answers may be found, piece by piece, if doctors can be persuaded to be more interested in long-term follow-up and the social consequences of illness (including the consequences of their treatment) and social scientists to be more interested in health as a variable in life patterns and social behaviour.

Approached from the viewpoint of persistent class and regional variation and inequality, a related research need emerges—for the detailed documentation and analysis of the many facets of everyday experience and exposure of individuals living in different physical, economic and cultural environments and micro-environments. Within such environmental milieux we need to put together those influences and processes which are frequently studied separately—the health-related experience and behaviour of individuals spanning their everyday activities of diet, exercise, income and expenditure and work; their formal and informal educational and cultural exposure to ideas about health, disease and the use of services; the level and quality of health-related services; and the processes which filter individuals from different family, class, and cultural backgrounds into the social, economic, and geographical positions which influence the next stages of their lives. Such studies need to start from individuals in their social and environmental settings, chart the pathways, and then to monitor them with a range of social science and medical viewpoints. Following such a procedure patterns of association can be built up by the combination and comparison of individual histories; whereas with our usual procedure of working from aggregated data the individual has already been lost. Essentially this means long-term studies of selected communities, not solely or even mainly on a data-bank basis, but by a series of focused studies within the same settings which are capable of being related to each other conceptually and analytically.

No structural base exists for the establishment and maintenance of such long-term, community-based, inter-disciplinary studies. Starting from secondary schools, and intensified through the Universities, knowledge is transmitted and developed through individual disciplines, those closest to each other emphasizing their identity against their disciplinary neighbours. Careers are pursued and gained within disciplines. Professional development and demarcation reinforce the boundaries. Within medicine research is pursued within services and specialties which are separately administered and financed; the main over-arching medical discipline, community medicine, occupies a precarious position within the medical schools invariably pressured into a medical rather than a social science approach in order to demonstrate its relevance to clinical medicine. Social scientists have no organizational base within the medical schools and the health services and, apart from occasional forays into health, find it easier to pursue their research interests in other fields. The organization of Research Councils follows the same disciplinary pattern, their main interest and funding being devoted to the care of their own disciplines. There are, of course, exceptions and there has been some growth in the last two decades of social scientific medical collaboration. The Royal Commission on the NHS recognized the need, in part, by recommending the establishment of an Institute for Health Services Research. Given the absence of a structural, administrative and funding base for long-term community research of an inter-disciplinary nature, it is not surprising that more attention has been paid to the parts rather than the whole. On the specific question of child health Blaxter commented:

A great deal of effort has gone into the task of proving, again and again, that these socially-associated differences in the health status of children do exist: almost as if this were something that society did not wish to believe, and had to rediscover at regular intervals. To continue to prove, however, that children's health and development differ according to the occupational social class of their father makes little impact upon the task of explaining why this should be so.

These comments could justifiably be extended well beyond the problems of child health.

3

Health beliefs, and health
and illness behaviour

Doctors spend many years acquiring a comprehensive compendium of knowledge about physiological, biochemical, and psychological facts and events and a distinctive method of organizing that knowledge into states, processes and syndromes. At the end of their training they have learnt how to obtain data from patients about their symptoms, to conduct physical examinations, to supplement the patient's report with other visible and tangible information, and to request investigations about internal substances and processes invisible both to them and to the patient. They then organize the available data to correspond with learnt patterns signifying specific diseases and physiological processes. Their objective is also specific, to link data patterns with acquired knowledge of causes and treatments.

This is one way of assembling and interpreting data relevant to illness. Whilst uncertainty and judgement are involved, and whilst the data deemed relevant, and their diagnostic and treatment significance may change from decade to decade, the basic principles are more permanent and constitute modern scientific medicine.

In an educated society with its developed systems of communication some patients may have learnt some of this store of medical knowledge and they may glean in various ways part of the special information about their own body and mind acquired by the doctor in the course of his examinations and investigations. But there is no *a priori* reason to assume that they view illness, its causes and treatment, in the same way, or with similar objectives. If they did, doctors would have less cause to complain that patients presented with trivial complaints or that they delayed too long after the onset of symptoms before seeking medical advice. The medical-sociological literature is replete with examples of the conflicting values and behaviour of patients and their doctors (Stimson, 1976; Davis and Horobin, 1976; Strong, 1980; Stimson and Webb, 1975; Robinson, 1973; Osofsky, 1968; Voysey, 1975; and Byrne and Long, 1976). They report the unwillingness/inability of doctors to communicate freely to patients; misunderstanding of motives and statements in consultations; deliberate termination of symptom-reporting deemed to be irrelevant to the medically-defined objective; the development of techniques for terminating consultations; and on the other hand, patients presenting illness symptoms to obtain discussion of non-medical problems, withholding information, being unable to judge when consultation is appropriate, making unnecessarily urgent demands, denying illness, etc. There are many possible explanations for both the doctors' and patients' behaviour or their account of each other's behaviour; on the one hand pressure of work and the need to control the use of time, the desire to maintain medical authority, impatience with wordy irrelevancy or definition of a problem as being outwith medical competence; and on the other, lack of experience or confidence, inability to express needs clearly, fear or distrust of authority, or desire to place responsibility upon someone else's shoulders. Such explanations are clearly possible or likely in many instances. There is, however, a more general explanation stemming from the differences in the position and objectives of lay and professional persons.

We have become accustomed to accept and understand that members of 'pre-scientific' societies or historical periods have different ideas about the causes and nature of illness. Social anthropologists and medical historians have documented lay attitudes and behaviour in relation to illness and have demonstrated how ideas about the causes of illness proceed out of the general culture and cosmology of a society. Discussing the logic of African science and witchcraft Max Gluckman (1944) recounts the story of an educated African teacher, whose child had died of typhus, and who claimed that the child had been killed by a witch. In response to scientific medical denials of such a cause, he replied 'I knew that typhus was caused by a louse from a person ill with typhus which gave my child typhus, and that he died of typhus, but why did the louse go to my child and not to the other children with whom he was playing?' Gluckman argued that this teacher and others he describes were responding to the question 'Why misfortune to me?' and that illness was one category, albeit a separate category, of misfortune, which had to be explained within the general belief system applying to all misfortunes. Both Gluckman and Evans-Pritchard (1937) in his study of Zande magic and sorcery, make the point that such explanations account, economically, for two related events, both the disease and the particular individual. 'We have no explanation of why the two chains of causation intersected at a certain time and in a certain place, because there is no interdependence between them' (Evans-Pritchard, 1937). Where, as in so many societies, witches are malevolent neighbours, the chain of causation goes back further and illness finds its ultimate cause in social relationships.

Winslow (1967) in a fascinating historical review of epidemic disease documents the relationship between social structure, general causal theories, and the origins of illness. Perhaps the clearest relationship emerges in those societies, pre-literate and with primitive technology in which all inexplicable or change events were attributable to demons. The propitiation of the demons, and the avoidance of illness or misfortune entailed the performance of acts, and conformity to rules which frequently had a social or political content. Winslow distinguishes one set of theories of particular social significance in that the demons or gods were not essentially malign or erratic but retributive or just. Illness was the punishment for disobedience to moral or social laws. The threat of illness was thus an additional inducement to religious and legal conformity and, as in Leviticus and Deuteronomy, to maintain the rules of hygiene and of social relationships.

I shall discuss three sets of thought, from three societies, about the causes and classification of health and illness and about the behaviour culturally required of patients. My purpose is to show, not only that systems of thought other than western scientific medicine, have developed rules for the identification, diagnosis, and treatment of illness and for the behaviour of sick persons but

47

that rules are normally referable back to the technology and social relationships existing within that society.

The Gnau villagers of New Guinea studied by Gilbert Lewis (1976) do not have a term such as 'illness' which clearly demarcates bodily from other misfortunes. The word they use for illness means bad or undesired and can be applied to many other states and events. They do however have words to describe sub-categories—they differentiate acute critical illness, using a word having overtones of death, from long-standing disorders for which they have a word, wretched or ruined, which is the same as the word for 'old'. They also distinguish separately illness of the whole or self, from illness of parts of the body. They could describe pains or physiological disorders (symptoms) but did not have a classification of disease names. Instead they were more likely to refer to a cause which, being external to the individual, did not require a description in bodily terms. 'Cause and remedy were to be revealed by other evidence than that of the body's state' and particularly in the malevolence of evil spirits, the enmity of neighbours or the breaking of socially-accepted norms of behaviour.

The individual in this society did not need a doctor to diagnose illness—he was himself the best judge of whether he was ill. He demonstrated his diagnosis conspicuously by withdrawal into a passive and wretched state, shunning company and conversation, lying apart, begriming himself with dirt and ashes, rejecting normal foods, and even erecting a physical barrier between himself and others. This is conventional behaviour, modelled upon common reactions to severe illness, but it also has a symbolic, culturally-defined significance. Thus, such 'illness behaviour' is simultaneously the assumption of a new social status as a sick person, and a request for treatment by his fellows, for he is not himself responsible for his own treatment.

The Gnau do acknowledge a positive concept of health, something akin to 'well-being' which is related to the notion of resistance and derived partially from conformity to rules of prudent behaviour.

My second example is drawn from the work of Claudine Herzlich (1973) who based her analysis upon interviews in

France in the 1960s with a professional or middle-class and mainly Parisian sample. Herzlich attempted to draw out of lengthy discursive interview material the underlying conceptions of health and illness and the behavioural orientations to illness held by her respondents. She identified three common but different definitions of health. The first definition, which she called 'health-in-a-vacuum', was a passive or negative definition amounting to the absence of illness and contrasted with a frequently-used concept 'equilibrium', perhaps best described in English as well-being, positive real health, an abundance of bodily potential, which was simultaneously a subjective feeling and a norm of what ought to be. It was the actualization of the third type of definition used by her respondents, which she called 'a reserve of health', which being an organic/biological characteristic of the individual, could be seen as a capital asset and the source of resistance to disease. In contrast to health, which was an attribute of the individual, illness appeared as an external thing, a threat to the individual from outside himself, and a consequence of the way of life, seen by these Parisians as the unnatural and cumulatively toxic state of modern urban living. 'Hygiene' or health behaviour, seen largely in terms of good food, fresh air and sleep, was a potentially effective response to, and the necessary accompaniment of, their essentially unhealthy way of life. They were, of course, familiar with the symptoms of illnesses and with medical concepts of disease but, although physical symptoms took them to a doctor, illness was also a subjective state and could not be reduced to its purely physical aspects. Through its imposition of inactivity, the experience of illness went beyond the physical level and affected their whole life, their work and other roles, their independence, their relationship with others, and their social status. Illness was thus defined by subjective awareness and by its effects rather than by physical symptoms and causes. Apart from their medical-scientific meanings, illnesses were also classified by their relationship to the individual in terms of seriousness, curability and pain.

Herzlich also identified different psychological reactions to illness; the denial of illness and resistance by willpower to its consequences; the (temporary) acceptance of illness and the active participation in cure by working at it; and a different form of acceptance which stressed its beneficial qualities in personal liberation from customary roles and in enrichment of the individual.

My third example draws on recorded interviews by Mildred Blaxter and Elizabeth Paterson (1980) with two generations of Aberdeen women, where mother and daughter were both in Social Classes IV and V and both had been resident in Aberdeen since the daughter's birth. These informants, and particularly the mothers, are the product of a very disadvantaged social and medical history. The investigators found little evidence of any concept of positive health. For these mothers health was mainly seen as an absence of illness, of pain, or of the need for medical attention and hospitalization. There was, however, some evidence of a concept of basic or underlying health. They would frequently characterize themselves as 'healthy except for . . .' and the exceptions would be current but specific illnesses and past illnesses which had now disappeared or had been stabilized. Such exceptions could sometimes be serious illnesses but frequently referred to problems affecting a part of the body—sinus problems, shoulder pain, defective eyesight. A major criterion of health was whether they were able to continue their normal activity and particularly their work.

Illness consisted of the 'dreaded illnesses' of tuberculosis, polio, cancer, leukaemia, cerebral haemorrhage, and heart disease, but also of chronic disabling conditions, those requiring heavy medication or restricted activity. Common illnesses, coughs, colds, infections, sinus problems, and shoulder pain, were not seen as affecting health status. The women also accepted as non-illnesses conditions relating to a particular stage in the life cycle, the 'inevitable' illnesses of children growing up or of adults growing old, which were seen as part of a natural process.

Lack of a concept of positive health was reflected in an antipathy to preventive health measures. The older generation did place emphasis on 'proper' food, plenty of sleep, fresh air, and 'a warm clean bed', but there was scepticism or even fatalism about the benefits of preventive medicine or dentistry. 'If your kids are healthy, they're healthy. If they're going to be ill, they'll be ill.'

Concepts of causation however were elaborate and subtle, particularly in the older generation. Illnesses were rarely mentioned without imputed cause. Theories of multiple causation and chains of cause were often used involving combinations of environmental conditions, constitution, heredity and strain in whole family health histories over generations.

The response to illness often contained moral overtones, illness being seen as a state of mind which should be resisted. Keeping going, not lying down to it, not letting it get you down, carrying on work, going to school, were recipes against illness and the themes of mind over matter and moral failure frequently occurred. This was associated with refusal to accept symptoms and with normalization of recurrent conditions.

These three examples, drawn from diverse cultural settings, illustrate the extremes of different orientations to health and illness; different from each other and, more important for my purpose, different from those acquired by doctors in their long and expensive training.

The existence of this discrepancy between the health beliefs and practices of the Gnau and those of western scientific medicine should not surprise us. Over the last 20 years anthropologists have become increasingly interested in health and illness and they have provided us with literally hundreds of detailed ethnographies. In societies such as the Gnau, which have remained isolated from western contact until comparatively recently, it has been possible to describe a single self-contained system of beliefs and practices. Such societies are rare, and instead of 'pure' disease concepts uniquely bound to a specific cultural matrix, it is more usual to find two or three sets of disease concepts partly side by side, partly intermingled. The first set stems from folk medicine, traditional to all societies. The second set has its origins in organized traditional medicine, for example Ayurvedic and Uniani medicine in India. The third, and increasingly dominant set, stems from western scientific medicine. There is now an impressive body of evidence showing that dual and sometimes triple systems can and do exist side by side. For example, Leslie (1976) and Bhatia (1971, 1973, 1974) have demonstrated the simultaneous existence of folk, Ayurvedic and western beliefs and practices in various parts of India. In a similar way Fabrega (1974) has shown that Maya concepts intermingle Ladino and western theories of disease. Dual systems involving folk and western medicine have been extensively studied by Maclean (1971) in Nigeria, Press (1969) in Bolivia, Lieban (1976) in the Philippines and Rubel and Spicer (1977) in Mexican-American communities. More recent examples of this interesting work can regularly be found in the medical anthropology section of *Social Science and Medicine*. From this accumulated work it is not only clear that the phenomenon is widespread throughout the developing world, it is also extremely complex and cannot be understood in simple terms of 'pragmatism'. It is necessary to examine the way in which patients perceive and evaluate a host of factors, beginning with their beliefs in the efficacy of treatment offered by a variety of healers and their overall relationships with these healers. Given this body of evidence it is surprising that we often make the mistake of assuming that the situation is entirely different in western or industrial societies. The prevailing view is that people who are ill will automatically enter the orbit dominated by professionally trained doctors. Leslie (1976, p. 375) provides an emphatic refutation of this view:

In the United States and other industrial countries, laymen and specialists assume that a single cosmopolitan medical system exists, with comprehensive jurisdiction in all matters of health: a hierarchy of paramedical specialists dominated by physicians; standard therapeutic techniques and ways of generating new skills and knowledge. In fact, the medical system is a pluralistic network of different kinds of physicians, dentists, clinical psychologists, chiropractors, health food experts, yoga teachers, spirit curers, druggists, Chinese herbalists, and so on. The health concepts of a Puerto Rican worker in New York City, the curers he consults and the therapies he receives, differ from those of the Chinese laundryman or the Jewish clerk. They in turn differ from the middle class believers in Christian Science or logical positivism.

The cultural and medical pluralism which Leslie identifies in the USA is undoubtedly greater than that confronting Herzlich and Blaxter and Paterson in their French and Scottish samples. However, in both of these studies we have seen examples of 'folk' beliefs and practices which do not coincide with 'official' medicine. For me as a medical sociologist it is highly gratifying that this discrepancy is beginning to be noticed by doctors themselves. In a recente ditorial comment Dr Neil Stevenson (1980), an East Anglian GP, acknowledged that his patients regularly confronted him with definition sof illness different from those for which he had been trained:

> Their descriptions of their complaints reveal a set of concepts quite foreign to cosmopolitan medicine. They speak of 'a chill' which may be general in its effect on the body or centred on some specific organ such as the stomach or kidneys, of a state of 'biliousness', 'indigestion', 'eye strain', 'fibrositis'. The familiarity of such ideas blinds many physicians to the fact that they are rooted in a system of folk medical concepts and are alien to the cosmopolitan medical system.

Western scientific medicine is only decades away from the traditional, largely ineffectual, tincture-of-rhubarb formulations of the old family doctor. Occasional sociological studies of medical work, indeed, remind us that magical elements continue to exist in orthodox medicine (Roth, 1957; Posner, 1977). The absorption into popular thought of what has become an enormously complex structure of knowledge, interpretations, and perspectives and which is constantly elaborated by academic and commercial research must be partial or even fragmentary. Such knowledge as lay persons possess comes rarely from organized teaching but by word of mouth from relatives and friends, from the person's own limited contacts with medicine, from newspaper and magazine articles, and from radio and television (frequently over-dramatized and focusing disproportionately upon the visible and the spectacular). If we accept that there is some unity of thought and some link between thought and action in the lives of social groups (and the anthropologists provide impressive evidence to this effect from pre-literate and agricultural societies) then it is likely that illness behaviour reflects the system of thought and belief. Stimson (1976) asked general practitioners to describe patients who caused them most trouble. The troublesome patients included those who present feeling ill, with vague symptoms, who cannot judge when to consult, who vaguely present problems, do not accept limits to the doctor's skills, who do not want to get better or who deny illness. The gap in knowledge base is important, between the doctor's professional training and experience and the patient's limited knowledge of what the doctor knows and does. Blaxter and Paterson found that, in relation to the illnesses and health problems of young children, many women did not know what to treat seriously. Some were anxious as a result.

The implicit assumption that there is only one set of meanings attached to health and only one true medicine may lead to mis-interpretation of patients' behaviour. Entering the medical field only a few years after war service in the army I was intrigued to hear patients who did not keep a clinic appointment described as 'defaulters'. To me the term had overtones of soldiers absent without leave turning up on parade for morning punishment. It seemed possible to me that women did not understand the impersonal rituals to which they were subjected at ante-natal clinics and did not share medical belief in intensive ante-natal care. Rather than regarding them as defaulters it would have been profitable to discover their views, to ask how far the behaviour reflected failures of communication and to restructure clinic routines accordingly. A generation later it is interesting to note Macintyre's (1980) finding from her interviews with primi-gravidae that 'few of the women had ever given any thought to, or been given specific information about, the purpose of ante-natal care which was something that seemed to be taken for granted'.

In her study of patients and their doctors Cartwright summed up patients' ideas about a good family doctor as someone who would know them by name if he met them in the street, whose relationship with them was friendly rather than businesslike, someone with whom they could discuss a personal, and not strictly medical, problem and who was good about explaining things to them fully. Such findings are widespread. Stimson and Webb found that complaints about doctors derived more from failures of relationship than from technical failures (although patients' reports often associated the two). Blaxter and Paterson also report that the qualities admired in general practitioners were those of manner, personality, availability, and willingness to spend time on their patients. They further comment: 'It was notable how little the actual content of the service, in terms of diagnosis and treatment, was stressed positively as a favourable feature.' Patients' ability to judge technical competence and to make comparisons between doctors must be limited and to that extent the notion of (informed) choice is illusory, but there is the additional point that subjectively their illnesses mean something to them beyond the purely medical and the qualities they admire in a personal doctor are most likely to satisfy their subjective needs.

Knowledge, however, is only one component in a cultural difference. In each of the three examples illness had additional connotations and consequences, and particularly the possible cessation of or restrictions on customary activity. Herzlich's patients interpreted illness by its consequences, by the role-change and status and identity problems it engendered. Both for the Parisian middle-class and the Aberdeen working-class the subjective symptoms went beyond the objective disorder and could be seen as moral failure leading them to deny symptoms, to resist the status of patient and the passivity implicit in the sick role. Alternatively, Herzlich claims, the importance of the subjective state might lead them to oppose the doctor's judgement that they have 'nothing wrong with them' with convictions about changes in their mood and behaviour. The recent controversy about the over-technological management of pregnancy and childbirth stems largely from the emotional significance which women attach to maternity and parenthood. The movement towards self care (Williamson and Danaher, 1978) and the growth of mutual-aid groups of persons suffering from a common affliction (Robinson, 1977) are responses to similarly felt needs.

Postitive health is an elusive concept. Lewis appeared to find it among the Gnau where it was related to ideas of resistance and of conformity to rules of prudence by which health may be preserved. Herzlich's 'reserve of health' and 'equilibrium' or well-being had similar connotations. It appeared to be virtually absent in Aberdeen women from semi-skilled and unskilled working-class backgrounds. Behavioural evidence relating to smoking, diet, exercise, and dental care suggest that the idea of disease-prevention and perhaps of health maintenance is more prevalent in the middle- and professional-classes. The apparent reversal in ischaemic heart disease in recent decades, from being a primarily middle-class to a primarily lower-class disease, if not due to changes in diagnosis and errors of classification, suggests differential experience of and rates of adaptation to changing standards of living and styles of life. How far middle-class behaviour is a direct response to knowledge of health risks can only be a matter of judgement. Askham's (1975) study of family formation suggests a degree of unity in planning behaviour, individual family planning behaviour being strongly associated with similar behaviour in other spheres of social and economic activity. She concluded that such behaviour stemmed from similar pressures and experiences rather than from a cultural tradition. This may also be true of positive health.

Unlike the Azande and the Gnau we are members of a pluralist society composed of sub-groups differing in their social position, education, and way of life and who, from those positions experience and perceive our worlds in different ways. The Aberdeen women who lived throughout their lives in one city and one social stratum are likely to differ in many ways, including their orientation to health and illness, from similar groups brought up in London or Glasgow and from those who, born in Aberdeen, moved into a different stratum or geographical environment. The current expansion of the oil industry in Aberdeen and the influx of foreign oil workers, particularly Americans, is providing a number of examples of the way in which different cultural expectations are resulting in new demands on the health services. The emerging pattern awaits comprehensive study but it is already evident that the incoming workers and their families are responsible for dramatic increases in the work loads of hospital colleagues responsible for paediatric, orthodontic and psychiatric services. The medico-social multiplications of off-shore oil work have been explored by Morrice and Taylor (1978) and they have found it useful to introduce the concept of the 'intermittent husband syndrome' to characterize the psychiatric sequelae. As far as dental services and particularly orthodontics, are concerned it is clear that the incoming oil families were initially responsible for the increased demand but the higher expectations have now spread, primarily through the schools, to the indigenous population. In an area of the country with high levels of tooth decay and total extraction, often in preparation for weddings, this represents a sharp break with traditional practice (Bloor et al, 1978).

The notion of a social structure, a position within that structure and a set of ideas whose nature and origin can be related back to structure and position, has been most developed by anthropologists working in pre-literature or non-industrial societies. For many years sociologists teaching health and illness behaviour to their students relied on the anthropological literature and a few American studies (Koss, 1954; Rainwater, 1960, 1968) because of the almost total absence of comparable research in the UK. Information about behaviour can be gleaned from social surveys (and especially the work of Ann Cartwright) and from studies focused upon a medically-recognized problems such as over-use or under-use of health services. Much work was done from the 1960s onwards on hospitals and residential institutions relating institutional structure to patients' perception and behaviour. There is, however, still a massive gap in our knowledge which is only slowly being rectified. Only very tentatively can we provide answers to such questions as: how does life and experience in particular environments (class, age, sex, education, urban/rural residence, etc.) produce differing patterns of belief and behaviour? Do sub-cultural and 'official' ideologies (sets of ideas) co-exist side-by-side in the individual? If so, how are they drawn upon in different illness situations? How do they affect use of the services and communication with doctors and other health personnel? What is the extent and influence of lay sources of advice, referral and treatment? Is there a tendency to convergence between social groups in beliefs, knowledge, and behaviour? How far are differences due to the organization of care? We are even less able to check the validity and relevance of Herzlich's elegant classifications of health and illness behaviour to British populations.

Many sociologists are now interested in 'ethno-medicine' (see, for example, the latest (Arber, 1978) edition of *Medical Sociology in Britain: a register of research and teaching*). The bulk of such work is focused upon particular illnesses or health-service problems and it is possible that the accumulation of such studies will eventually permit a more comprehensive conceptual synthesis.

To the extent, however, that it is based upon patients in contact with services and thus abstracted from their daily environment, it deals with the behavioural consequences rather than the origins of ideas and behaviour. What is required are intensive studies of small samples of different population groups who have not already defined themselves, or been defined by others, as ill. They should ideally be prospective rather than retrospective, they should experiment with various methods of data collection, and they should cover a range of social groups representing different social classes, ages and areas of residence.

The reasons for our current lack of fundamental knowledge and research are undoubtedly complex—as with most gaps in knowledge. It is perhaps too easy to blame funding agencies, although it is true that research of this kind, dealing with social structures, ideas and non-patients seems too remote from the business end of the health services to attract enthusiastic funding. Fashions in sociology are also contributory. The sociologists who entered the medical field in large numbers in the 1960s and early 1970s were heavily pre-occupied with deviance, labelling, and the influence of professionals and of medical institutions on the creation of illness, just as sociologists of crime were more interested in the creation of delinquent careers by police and agents of social control than in the sources of delinquent behaviour in the community. I now see it as one of those fundamental areas of research, equivalent to much medically-relevant laboratory research in the natural sciences, which requires patient and long-term development and accumulation, interesting in its own right and basic to the provision of socially appropriate services and to health promotion.

4

The profession of medicine

To members of the medical profession, medicine has two essential meanings. Firstly it is a body of knowledge a set of skills, and a technology devoted to the understanding of health and illness and to the identification, diagnosis and treatment of disease. Secondly it is an organized profession characterized by a common initial training, self-organized entrance rules and codes of conduct and it is differentiated by specialist skills in the diagnosis and treatment of illness and by differing role-relationships towards other members of the profession and towards patients. Individual members will emphasize different aspects of this body of knowledge/skills and of their professional organization, according to their own position and status—as junior doctors obtaining membership qualifications, as single-handed general practitioners, as hospital consultants, or community medicine specialists.

Sociologists have studied medicine and medical work more fully than any other profession or professional activity. One major reason has been its availability for study. In recent years many doctors and medical organizations have invited sociologists to study their work or have tolerated their presence as observers. Certain features of medicine, however, have particularly attracted sociologists and I deal with three of them below.

MEDICINE AS A PROFESSION

With the same intensity that doctors might dispute the definition of alcoholism, sociologists used to argue about the nature of a profession. How did a profession differ from a trade or occupation? At what stage in its progression, by virtue of which newly acquired property, did an aspiring occupational group attain the dignity of professional status? Early work, derived from considering the claims of the church, medicine, and the law, and perhaps naively accepting the rhetoric of the professions themselves, attached importance to such ideas as a sense of vocation or calling as opposed to the desire to earn money, to selflessness beyond the call of duty, to the adoption of ethical codes which gave precedence to the client's interest over those of the practitioner or which regulated the conduct of its members towards each other and to the public, or to the length of preparation or training. Medicine was one of the very few classical professions and hence a possible source of enlightenment about the nature of profession itself.

The flood of new professions in the post-war world overwhelmed sociological naivete and most sociologists would now be prepared to accept a definition of a profession which contained no mention of ethics, trust, vocation, complex skills, or lengthy training, regarding these as the rhetoric or propaganda used by the profession to establish its professional status rather than something intrinsic to the nature of professions as such (Roth, 1974). Instead they would emphasize the concept of autonomy— the legitimated freedom to define the nature of the work, to establish the content of training and the requirements for entry, to control the quality of work, to operate disciplinary procedures for infringement of membership rules, and to exclude the claims of others to compete in the same field. The other components, the length of training, the ethical codes, and the predominance of the client's interests, are regarded as important, but only in the intermediate sense that they have persuaded (or in the case of would-be professions are likely to persuade) the public and the state to approve or legitimate their claim to authority.

Medicine, in this country primarily through the powers exercised by the General Medical Council, possesses these legitimated freedoms. The frequent rhetorical appeal to Hippocrates and Galen is misleading however in implying the age-long professional position of medicine. It is not merely that, according to McKeown (1976), doctors were likely to have killed more patients than they saved until the late nineteenth century, it is also that medicine in the UK did not professionalize in the strict sense mentioned above until the middle of the nineteenth century. Gill's (1976) analysis of the development of the medical profession in the UK demonstrates that, whilst the Act of 1858 regulated the rivalry of physicians, surgeons, and apothecaries it was not until well into the twentieth century that a single profession of medicine was established with monopolistic control over treatment and a general public acceptance of the profession's claim to competence.

Other professionals co-exist with doctors in the health field. Each has its own title, its field of practice and its professional organization. Once called ancillary staff or paramedical workers, they are now 'professions complementary to medicine'. Terminological confusion abounds. We talk of the Medical Research Council, not the Health Research Council, although the common topic of research is health, not medicine, and although most MRC professional staff are not medically qualified. We talk of medical problems when we mean health problems and we excuse individuals from duties on medical grounds. We do so because ultimately in our society problems cannot be accepted as health problems, or ill-health be regarded as significant, unless legitimated by medical expertise. Freidson (1970) accurately entitled one of his books *Professional Dominance: The social structure of medical care* for his analysis demonstrates that of all the 'health professions', the profession of medicine is dominant.

This means that all the work done by other occupations and related to the service of the patient is subject to the order of the physician. The profession alone is held competent to diagnose illness, treat or direct the treatment of illness, and evaluate the service. Without medical authorisation, little can be done for the patient by paraprofessional workers. The client's medication, diet, excretion, and recreation are all subject to medical orders. So is the information given to the patient. By and large, without medical authorisation, paramedical workers are not supposed to communicate anything of significance to the patient about what his illness is, how it will be treated, and what are the chances for improvement.

Freidson claims that,

with the exception of dentistry the only occupation that is truly autonomous is medicine itself. It has the authority to direct and evaluate the work of others without in turn being subject to formal direction and evaluation by them.

As far as health is concerned such dominance does not stop at the boundaries of the organized health system.

To put it more bluntly, teachers, social workers, ministers and others outside the medical division of labour refer to physicians and communicate information about the client to them, but physicians are not likely either to refer clients to them or to provide them with the results of medical investigations.

Work, and the institutions within which work is organized, are so central to the everyday life and welfare of a society, and exercise such influence upon the political and social structure, that they are inevitably and rightly important to the sociologist (Johnson, 1972; Hughes, 1958). And this must also apply, a fortiori to the idea of profession, a form of working organization characteristic of a complex industrial or post-industrial society. What significance does it have for the health system and the health professions?

Some of the specific implications of the dominant authority of medicine within the health system are discussed more extensively elsewhere in this volume—in particular the influence of medicine upon the concept of health and upon decision-making about health service priorities.

Perhaps most important in the context of the National Health Service is its impact upon other health service occupations and the organization of effective working relationships. If highly developed skills and an ethical commitment to the client were, as previously thought, the essential components of profession, the re-negotiation of roles to bring service into line with changing health problems and technology would be relatively simple. If however Freison's analysis is correct (and most sociologists would only disagree with details rather than the substance of his argument) the crucial feature of professionalism is autonomy and its pervasiveness.

The profession has been able to determine how many physicians are trained, who is selected to be trained, how they are to be trained and who is to be licensed and thus to work. In that way it has controlled the labour market for its services. Furthermore, it has exercised supervisory power over a growing array of technical workers—the para-professional workers who may not work without authorisation or whose products (like laboratory analyses, X-rays) are unusable by anyone but physicians. In that way it has dominated a division of labour. Its control both restricts the supply of its own labour and subordinates related labour in the institutions in which its members work. (Freidson in Stacey et al, 1977).

Other professionalizing occupations, differentiating themselves from medicine and other occupations, are seeking a similar degree of control over their work. Medicine, however, is already entrenched, has legal responsibility for treatment, and controls access to patients. The Royal Commission on the NHS quotes BMA evidence on this point:

No doctor fails to recognise the necessity of co-operation with the nursing profession and with other medical workers. But this does not mean that the doctor should in any way hand over his control of the clinical decisions concerning the treatment of his patients to anyone else or to a group or team. (Royal Commission, 1979).

However, in an increasingly complex health industry, necessarily organized on bureaucratic principles, individuals, specialist groups, professional associations, and unions bargain and negotiate for position on the basis of their necessary participation in joint activities. The doctor is neither the employer nor the inevitable leader. The Royal Commission recognized that the leadership problem arose in its most acute form in multidisciplinary clinical teams. In practice and, at this moment in time, the question can frequently be settled by agreement between individuals on an ad hoc basis, a point which emerges from Goldie's (1976) study of relationships between psychiatrists, social workers, and clinical psychologists. Goldie comments, however, that

the meaning of professionalisation may be quite different to the membership of a profession compared with the aims, ambitions and activities of the various office holders and 'spokesmen' of a particular professional association.

Where, as in social work, a considerable proportion of a profession practise outside the health field, 'secession' and subsequent bargaining from an independent position may be possible. For others, the process of inter-professional accommodation has begun with consensus management, functional management, joint consultation, and boundary demarcation. The very considerable body of sociological research on what the Royal Commission described as 'to put it mildly, a delicate matter', is likely to be multiplied as each of the many new professions attempts to secure its position.

Team work is a loose term referring generically to quite different organizational forms each having its intrinsic implication for the degrees of responsibility, consultation and autonomy of team members. Webb and Hobdell (1980) identify three main types, distinguished by the homogeneity or heterogeneity of skills and of tasks. The first, a collegial team is characterized by homogeneity of both skills and tasks and is exemplified by the relationship between general practitioners in a group practice. The second, a specialized collegial team, involves some members specializing in particular tasks but does not necessarily imply differences in skills or in hierarchical position. Specialization within a group practice or within a social work team would typify this model. Both organizational forms are familiar, conform with ideas about professional autonomy and individual responsibility and are relatively unproblematic. The third or complex team is heterogeneous in both skills and tasks, involving the notion that individuals with quite different skills should perform separate tasks within a combined enterprise, either in a hospital ward, a health centre or a more loosely organized community service. Many such tasks require co-ordination and the central issues in teamwork are who should be the co-ordinator, what degree of responsibility and accountability the co-ordinator should have for the outcome of the enterprise and what authority he should possess about the task performance of each member of the team, irrespective of professional affiliation. The problem is not solely one of individual autonomy, or even of professional autonomy (although these are clearly important) but of the differing degrees of hierarchical authority and task-standardization within each profession. Within medicine the degree of individual autonomy varies between general practice and hospital work, and within hospital medicine the degree of structuring varies between medical and surgical wards (Coser, 1958; Davies and Francis, 1976). A clear division of accountability takes place at the consultant level across all medical specialties in hospital work, although in some new and interesting developments within psychiatry, degrees of authority are consciously blurred

64

both between and within professions (Bloor, 1980). Recent developments in nursing, occurring contemporaneously with nurses' bid for higher professional status have, on the contrary, tended towards firmer hierarchical organization and line management with a more precise structuring and grading of tasks and the separation of management from nursing tasks. This has been described by Davies and Francis (1976) as 'professionalization without, *via* bureaucratization within'. The unification of social work into a single authority has tended in the same direction. The problems of inter-professional and inter-organizational collaboration that arise from such differences in professional organization have been clearly identified in a series of empirical studies of health authority/local government planning machinery by the Birmingham Institute of Local Government Studies (Norton and Rogers, 1977, 1980); other investigators (Ratoff et al, 1974; Reilly et al, 1977) have studied working arrangements between general practitioners and social workers and identify as a further source of tension their differing perception of patients' problems and the clash of priorities which arises for the social worker attached to a general practice but also having professional responsibilities to local authority colleagues.

The study of professions, professional organisation and inter-professional relationships in the health and social services feeds back into general sociological interest in occupations and organizations. It is however particularly pertinent to tensions in health service industrial relations and particularly so in view of the increasingly syndicalist nature of the NHS.

MEDICINE AS KNOWLEDGE AND SKILLS

Whilst the professional dominance of medicine derives from its success (and its relatively early success among the health professions) in securing legitimated autonomy over its work, a large part of its claim to such autonomy was based upon its parallel status as a scientific discipline. Whether or not Thomas McKeown was correct in claiming that the decline in mortality from infectious disease owed more to social improvement than to the application of medical science, it is undoubtedly true that medicine acquired its prestigious scientific reputation because of the almost unchallenged acceptance of that claim. Colin Dollery (1978), defending the contributions of medical science in a previous Rock Carling monograph, stated the claim rather dramatically as follows:

Some of the early achievements in the treatment of infectious disease were so miraculous as almost to surpass belief. They, literally, changed the world. The watch and wait while the pneumonia of a young adult progressed through crisis to lysis or death. The agony of a child with acute ostitis media, or worse still, osteomyelitis. The long-drawn-out vigil of the patient with pulmonary tuberculosis coughing away his life. Anti-bacterial chemotherapy made the cure of such scourges almost a matter of routine. It was a time of optimism. Science appeared to have the salvation of the world in its hand and mankind could look forward to an era of healthy ease and modest luxury. The budgets of the Medical Research Council and the National Institutes of Health increased exponentially and journalistic comment about medical research was almost always eulogistic.

However relevant or irrelevant the techniques of medical science were to the conquest of epidemic disease in the late nineteenth and early twentieth centuries, the scientific developments of this period and the more recent stream of discoveries in chemistry and biology laid the foundations of modern medical science with its infinitely more advanced understanding of bacteriological, physiological, and biochemical processes as they affect human disease and with its more powerful techniques for preventing and controlling disease and for relieving pain and suffering.

Part of that undoubtedly effective medical science has now become irrelevant in the developed world. Instances crop up from time to time when a previously common infectious disease, typhoid, smallpox, or diphtheria, is diagnosed late for the reason that, in modern British society, many doctors have never encountered the disease and fail to recognize symptoms which might well have been self-evident to an Edwardian layman. Two developments out of that earlier period of medicine continue substantially to influence the directions and the contribution of medical science.

1. They dictated the past development of scientific medicine and have established a particular image of medicine both in the

66

eyes of the profession and of the public. The body of knowledge accumulated in the last 150 years is socially situated—that is, it grew out of the social conditions of an industrializing economy and the living conditions and environment of a poorer society which pre-disposed to a particular constellation of diseases and ill-health. Those conditions and the illnesses they engendered have disappeared outside the countries of the Third World, but the very fact of their virtual eradication at the time when medical science was only decades away from the ineffectual or even lethal remedies of the mid and late nineteenth century gave medicine its scientific heroes and imbued medical education, medical institutions, and medical ambitions with concepts and approaches which are not obviously appropriate in contemporary conditions. Renée Fox (1976) describes a mural at the Institut Jules Bordet in Brussels honouring the distinguished medical scientist after whom the institute is named.

. . . the mural is a portrait of a scientist of gentlemanly origins and demeanor, a solo investigator, working in his laboratory at night in the anatomo-patho-logical and bacteriological era of medicine, and equipped only with his sense of vocation, his personal genius, and simple instruments.

Modern medical research differs from this Bordet image in fundamental respects. More than the style of the buildings, the haberdashery of its investi-gators, and the equipment it employs have changed. Modern research is char-acterized by a progressive division of labour, increasing specialization and pro-fessionalization. Biochemistry, rather than anatomy, pathology, or bacteriology, is the reigning basic medical science. The lone researcher is a relatively rare phenomenon. Increased knowledge, specialization, and the intricacy and expense of medical technology require that research be conducted by teams of investigators as a cooperative enterprise. The commitment to teamwork, however, is more than a rational recognition of the most practical way to proceed. Collaboration is considered to be morally as well as intellectually superior to an aloof, aristocratic individualism. Established, prestigious, com-fortably remunerated status-roles and careers exist. These are primarily in the university, but also in government and industry. They are not the prerogative of amateur gentlemen scholars. Rather, they are open to persons from wide-ranging social class backgrounds, primarily on the basis of their training and accomplishments.

The greater part of modern medical research is carried out within the framework of large, formal organizations that are essentially bureaucratic. These structures accommodate the changing configurations of medical science, including the rise of new disciplines and subfields, and shifts in the content or scope of basic and applied goals. Furthermore, medical researchers are linked to one another by informal scientific and collegial exchanges, mutually read publications, and membership in loosely organized professional societies.

Fox was deliberately emphasizing change but other sociologists have been struck by the similarities, by the preponderance of the laboratory sciences in medical education, the hospital as the virtually sole location of medical learning, the prestige accorded to natural-scientific methodologies and advances, the lowly status within medicine of specialties concerned with care rather than cure, the minimal role of behavioural sciences in medical education, the high proportion of resources devoted to hospital medicine and to research into, and the use of, drugs etc. These considerations have led many sociologists with varying degrees of disappointment, disapproval, or anger to reject the 'medical' or the 'disease' model of health and illness. One recent statement (Strauss, 1978), referring to American medical education, put the case as follows:

The major impediment to changing the dominant values in medical education to permit more emphasis on the importance of interpersonal relations is the orientation of faculty members who now hold positions of power and control in academic medicine. Most of these individuals were recruited or received academic tenure during the 1960s when society's support for science and technology was high. Most were valued for their investigative skills and/or the expertise they had attained in highly specialised aspects of disease diagnosis and treatment. Most are eminently well-qualified clinical specialists.

They have developed their expertise as clinical scientists in dealing with particular organs or diseases or techniques, not as clinical practitioners in relating to the people whose organs are diseased. They provide ideal role models as investigators and subspecialists. They create expectations and sanction the behavior of students in accordance with their own images. As a result medical students tend also to become preoccupied with the pathological, the unusual, the esoteric; with the disease or the diseased organ rather than the sick person. Students are rewarded by the clinical scientists who are their models, for their biological knowledge or technical skills. They are not rewarded for displaying inter-personal skills. They may even be chided if they seem to devote too much time or express too much concern for a patient. They learn to identify patients with challenging illnesses. . . . They think well of themselves when they devote their time to unusual pathology; they have a low self-esteem when they see only patients with common illnesses.

The case is often overstated and I wish to make my own position clear. I accept the benefits of medical science and medical technologists. Like those medical sociologists who attack doctors and hospitals I rush off to a doctor when I think I'm ill. Nor do I deny that most individual doctors care about their patients as persons or that some branches of medical practice put people, their perceived needs and emotions at the centre of their work. The 'medical model' criticism is not directed at individual doctors but at historical tendencies as general and impersonal as those which produce inflation, delinquency, or bureaucracy. The case is that the basic thrust and emphasis of medicine and of medical science needs up-dating.

Health resources can be directed towards different target populations. Behind each target population lies a different concept of health and of health policy as well as an appropriate set of techniques and a delivery system. These populations may be characterized along several dimensions:

> Sick/at risk/well
> Identified/unidentified
> Individuals/populations
> Acute/chronic illness
> Single/multiple conditions

Services appropriate for this range of populations and conditions may be characterized as

Developmental	Maintenance
Educational	Supportive
Screening	Environmental
Diagnostic	Preventive
Treatment	Restrictive

In most western countries the services are overwhelmingly diagnostic and treatment-oriented, and are best fitted to reach identified sick individuals and to deal with acute single conditions. Scientific medical research is focused predominantly on physiological, biomedical, neurological processes, and on techniques of pharmacological and surgical intervention. Criticism has, of course, been directed against the effectiveness, efficiency, or iatrogenic effects of this type of medicine from sources as diverse as Illich and Cochrane. It is however possible to mount a strong argument against the thrust of modern scientific medicine whilst acknowledging its undoubted success in the reduction of morbidity and mortality and its everyday contribution to the relief of pain and suffering.

Few critics of the disease model of health, Illich (1975) excepted, would wish to dispense with the benefits of those scientific discoveries and techniques which, as Dollery claimed, have 'literally, changed the world'. They are concerned that medicine developed a specific armamentarium at a particular point in history and that its possession and reinforcement over time have obscured the emergence of new needs for which that armamentarium is inappropriate. Kaplan (1964) discussing methods of inquiry formulated the 'Law of the Instrument': 'Give a small boy a hammer and he soon discovers that everything he encounters needs pounding'. The implication is that we now need other instruments more appropriate for achieving what Herzlich (1973) described as the 'reserve of health' and the feeling of equilibrium.

2. The second significant development stemming from medical scientific success in reducing mortality from infectious disease was the consolidation of the medical profession as the authority on matters of health and illness. Intellectually, administratively, legally, and morally the medical profession has assumed dominance in all health matters relative to other occupations. Because of the autonomy of a dominant profession to control the nature of its work, this has meant that, in effect, medicine has been able to define the boundaries of health and illness, to train entrants to the profession according to its concepts, scientific approaches, and techniques and to exercise an exclusive authority over the diagnosis and treatment of illness. The twofold corollary is that conceptual innovation about the nature of health and illness had to emerge within the profession and that other professionalizing occupations within the health field, as noted earlier, had to adjust themselves to the dominant ideology.

All long-established institutions practising in a changing world have to face the question of how to accommodate to innovation. The churches, the law, the universities, education generally, like medicine, have faced the question acutely in the last 150 years. Their ability to adapt, and the results of their adaptation, are conditional upon many factors—the scale and speed of social change and its implications for the product or service they have to offer, their vulnerability to competitors, the directness of pressure applied by external forces such as government, the public and other related organizations, the institutional structure in which they are embedded etc. Some have withered in influence because their 'product' has proved unadaptable. Medicine with its legal advantage over competitors, its life/death, health/illness product, its past scientific and clinical successes, its strong professional organization, faced problems of a different order—viz. the pace and degree of adaptation necessary to update its scientific ideology, its concepts of health and illness, its training methods and its internal organization to meet effectively the demand for health policies and types of health care arising out of new social conditions and associated patterns of health and illness. For this purpose some of the very strengths of traditional medicine—past successes, the prestige attached to proved scientific and technological approaches, the powerful institutions evolved to apply those approaches, and the need for all innovation to arise and grow within a single profession—were potential barriers to conceptual and organizational change. Discussing the need for radical change in medical education Margot Jeffreys (1976) pointed to the assumption that

if mortality and morbidity were to be further reduced, all doctors in training needed to acquire a knowledge of the growing mass of esoteric information concerning body systems. . . . The fallacy lies, I believe, in assuming that modalities and the human qualities which led to success in extending the frontiers of knowledge in micro-biology and laboratory-based scientific work, were also necessary for success in diagnosing, treating and managing illness in the community.

She identified the influence of the power-structure within the medical school as a potent factor in delaying the acceptance of a social science approach within medical education. 'Those most likely to favour a social science approach—that is, the psychiatrists, epidemiologists, social medicine experts and general practitioners —are generally low down in the medical school's "pecking order" of professional esteem.' To the list of disciplines and topics low in the pecking order she could well have added geriatrics, mental

retardation, nutrition, rehabilitation, health education, ophthal-
mology, dermatology, and family planning. In an established
unitary structure resistance occurs not only to imports from
outside the profession but also to those new approaches growing
up within the profession which do not conform to prevailing
emphases, and which call for diversion of already allocated
resources to other ends.

Many expressions of medical thought, in professional journals,
in the media, and in evidence to the Royal Commission on the
NHS give the impression that medicine is currently under siege.
There are indeed threats from several quarters to the traditionally
secure place of medicine with the health system. One is the threat
posed by expectations of continuous growth. This threat is
common to all sectors of the UK economy but is felt more
keenly by medicine because of its role as the initiator of health
system developments and because of the ever-so-gentle pressures
of the Health Departments for rationalization, medical audit, and
financial control. A second threat arises from within the medical
profession itself as specialties catering for newly-felt needs, backed
up by Health Department statements about priority, compete for
resources. A third threat comes from complementary professions,
and forces upon medicine the need for negotiation and accommodation, and the adoption of industrial relations machinery
hitherto confined to manufacture and commerce. Sociological
study and analysis of these simultaneous pressures has barely
begun but is likely to increase sharply as they are seen to affect
almost all corners of the health system. Earlier and rather naive
concepts of medical imperialism are likely to be replaced in such
analyses by a more complex formulation involving the idea of
boundary management between professions with different
definitions of need, based on different bodies of knowledge, and
each claiming the opportunity and the resources to exercise the
intrinsic skills implied by such definitions and scientific perspectives (see Strong, 1979).

MEDICINE AS A SYSTEM OF SOCIAL CONTROL

Social philosophers and social scientists are perennially concerned with the concept of social order. Given the vast number of individuals and family units, with different backgrounds and personalities and with a variety of biological, economic, emotional, and social needs, how is social interaction regulated to produce patterns of behaviour which transcend individual needs and allow members of society to have reasonable expectations of the behaviour of others? Consideration of this problem has produced theories, at the macro-social level, about the function of the state, about the role of economic classes in society, and about the rule of the law and the organs of government. All such theories involve the notion of rules of behaviour and power, the means whereby such rules are enforced. The formal systems are easy to identify in government, the law, the police, and the multiplicity of administrative agencies of a modern society. Since all individual actions, however, cannot be formally supervized and controlled, sociologists have examined the informal systems whereby consensus is inculcated, expectations created and infractions sanctioned. The socializing influences of the family, of formal and informal systems of education, of religious belief and organization, of economic and political organization, of art and the media of communication have been explored in a variety of cultural settings. Some of the major concepts of sociology, e.g. norms, beliefs, values, ideology, and culture have emerged from and been refined in these explorations, together with other concepts such as deviance, anomie, sanctions, and social control relating to the infraction and regulation of norms.

Social anthropologists and historians have demonstrated how, in pre-scientific societies rules of health behaviour tended to reinforce social norms; theories about the causation of disease attributing both epidemics or individual illness to violations of societal rules governing relationships and beliefs. For students of social control, modern medicine provides analytical problems of a different order.

Well individuals are expected to undertake a range of activities and responsibilities consonant with their age and position in

73

societies. Nonconformity to such expectations is a form of deviant behaviour which requires explanation, justification, or control. Persons who cannot, by reason of illness, carry out their normal responsibilities require some form of legitimation, and in a famous statement of the obligations of the sick role Parsons (1958) stipulated as one obligation the need to seek technically competent help and to co-operate in trying to get well. Given the position of medicine as the sole definer of sickness this makes the medical profession one of the arbiters of deviant behaviour. Refusal to define an individual as sick under these circumstances creates difficulties for the individual in his social and economic relations and leaves him open to other possible definitions such as lazy, criminal, or irresponsible. The obligation upon doctors to provide sickness certificates to employers and the social security system is the most common embodiment of the doctor's position in the system of social control.

If all diseases were clear-cut and organic, medicine's role in social control would be limited. Sociologists have noted however that the increasing acceptance of behavioural disturbance as illness has brought many other forms of potentially deviant behaviour within the medical orbit (Zola, 1972). Mental retardation, insanity, neurosis, homicide, suicide, shop-lifting, sexual behaviour, aggression, drug and alcohol 'abuse', and baby- and wife-battering, for example, have each come to be regarded to varying degrees and in certain circumstances either as illnesses or as problems susceptible to medical advice and treatment. The boundary lines between what is socially undesirable and what is sick behaviour in a medical sense are difficult to draw. The uncomfortable suspicion has been frequently voiced that some forms of medical diagnosis and labelling, particularly those relating to mental illness or insanity, are convenient means of locking away individuals whose behaviour is uncomfortable for society. Psychiatrists themselves are concerned about its use in the USSR as a means of silencing political critics. The situation is exacerbated by the fact that decision-rules for the diagnosis of illness are not so strict as those for determining criminal behaviour; nor are they so open to public view and judgement. It does not, however, require such extreme cases to make the point that the more medicine moves from technological intervention in organic conditions to the surveillance and modification of everyday behaviour, the more likely it is that it will be involved in controversial issues on which its motivation and authority can be challenged. This is an uncomfortable position for a profession which has based its claim to status and autonomy on scientific principles, and which has emphasized its freedom from political and social values.

Sociology has long confronted and never solved the question as to whether it should be a value-free science. In one sense the question is irrelevant in that, in practice, sociologists approach their subject with a range of overt or covert ideologies. Their attitudes towards medical-social control and 'the medicalization of everything' illustrate this political diversity. One strand of thought sees creeping medicalization much as left-wing politicians would see creeping capitalism. The privileged dominant profession is seen as extending its control, not merely over its rightful scientific domain but also over everyday life, and in so doing diverting attention away from political solutions to political problems (Navarro, 1977). Others (e.g. Conrad, 1979) treat it descriptively as an interesting empirical problem. Strong (1979) in the first sociological attack on the thesis of medicalization, is sceptical and views the whole thesis as a piece of sociological imperialism, an attempt by sociologists to stake out an alternative claim in the health field; he argues that if medicine itself were deliberately imperialistic the social model of health would be a better vehicle for expansion than the much abused medical model.

My own work on abortion (Illsley, 1976) suggests yet another interpretation. During the late nineteenth and the early twentieth century under the pressure of increasing child survival and population growth, the need for a highly-educated labour force to operate the new advanced technology, and the gradual involvement of women in non-household activity, a movement developed to control conception, to limit families and ultimately to terminate unwanted pregnancies. Many established institutions perceived this movement as a threat to traditional social values and to the institutions of marriage and the family. Considering the centrality of this topic to their professional field, gynaecologists took only a sporadic and rarely an initiatory role in the debate. Contraception received only the scantiest, if any, attention in medical education. Until the development of a chemical contraceptive, contraceptives were the commodities of hairdressers, slot-machines, and retail chemists. The professional associations of obstetricians and gynaecologists were equivocal on the moral issues and frequently condemnatory. Individual doctors, for the most part, left practice to a handful of specialists or to voluntary agencies and in counselling were prone to use their personal social and moral values as the source of their advice (Aitken-Swan, 1977). In refraining from what they saw as a moral debate they were upholding the scientific objectivity of their professional ethic, but, at the same time, were implicitly supporting established values and institutions.

The debate about abortion was the more embarrassing because gynaecologists were the occupational group legalized to perform the operation and to do it with maximum safety for the patient. Their refusal to carry out abortions or to campaign in their favour was therefore tantamount to a total prohibition on safe abortion. By refusing, and even more by notifying suspected abortions, they were acting as moral police. Nor was abortion always illegal so that in countries (e.g. Scotland) which had not passed anti-abortion laws, they were interpreting public welfare and upholding, not the law, but their professional rules and ideology.

Debate within the profession could not forever be avoided but, to be professionally acceptable, it had to be carried out in terms of medical science. Early research centred on the question of whether continuation might lead to maternal death or suicide. The linking of rubella to foetal malformations widened the grounds for abortion but retained the medical/biological character of the decision. The introduction of psychiatric criteria qualitatively changed the situation. The earlier psychiatric research examined such questions as whether continuation of pregnancy would exacerbate pre-existing psychosis or would pre-dispose to postpartum psychosis. Later research studied, and produced scientific justification for, abortion on the grounds of neurosis, personality defects, psychological vulnerability, etc. Since these were diagnostic or explanatory categories, conventionally used in clinical psychiatry, they could be held to constitute medical/ scientific grounds for abortion, but because they were loose in definition and infinitely stretchable they could also be used to justify on medical grounds the termination of an unwanted pregnancy which brought disturbance to the life of the mother. Psychiatrists were drawn with quite unusual frequency into decision-making—particularly in cases relating to young healthy girls where past obstetric complications or other somatic criteria were inapplicable. After the Abortion Act it has rarely proved necessary to refer a patient to the psychiatrist for an opinion.

I have chosen this example because it illustrates simultaneously several aspects of the relationship between medicine and prevailing social values. The role of gynaecologists as guardians of public morality was evident in the century preceding the Abortion Act. So also in the early research literature was the felt need to make decisions on medical-scientific grounds. In the decade preceding the Act, however, medicine was used to de-politicise the argument and to justify legislative change without needing to confront the moral, religious and political issues. At this point the diversity of disciplines subsumed under medicine and particularly the existence of behavioural medicine permitted conformity to changed social and political conditions without abandoning the value-free stance.

The way in which the introduction of medical criteria into a political or moral issue can serve to humanize and depoliticise the treatment of deviant behaviour has been noted by other sociologists (Zola, 1972). Conrad (1979) comments:

One of the most important functions of the disease model of alcoholism, and to a lesser extent, drug addiction is the secondary gain of removing blame from, and constructing a shield against condemnation of individuals for their deviant behaviour.

Strong (1979) points out that, contrary to the medicalization thesis, the medical profession has frequently and strenuously avoided entry into mainly social areas and has attempted to avoid responsibility for patient groups and conditions for which its techniques are inappropriate.

MEDICINE AS WORK

The attempt to understand medicine as a profession, as a science, an an agent of social control, to identify its distinctive approaches to the definition of health and illness, and to treatment, and to the intended and unintended consequences of its approaches for health care, and for the health system, has led sociologists into detailed studies of the working practices of medicine. Whilst for everyday purposes medicine can be regarded as a single occupation or profession distinguishable from other occupations such as law, accountancy, or nursing, it is exceptional in the variety of the tasks it performs and in the essential nature of those tasks. Except for their initial qualifications and their professional membership there is little in common between a pathologist, an obstetrician, a psychiatrist, a community medicine specialist, and a general practitioner. In the problems they handle, the knowledge and skills on which they draw, their working styles and their relationship to their patients/ clients psychiatrists may have more in common with social workers than with surgeons. Even within a single specialty such as psychiatry, there is extreme diversity in theoretical assumptions, relationships to patients, methods of treatment, work settings, types of patients, and working relationships with other professions and organizations. The range and variety of sociological research on medical work reflects the diversity of medicine. One major set of themes (Byrne and Long, 1976; Comaroff, 1976; McIntosh, 1977; Macintyre, 1976a, 1976b; Stimson and Webb, 1975; Strong, 1980) centres around the style and effectiveness of communication—methods of eliciting information and their implications for diagnosis and treatment; listening to patients as opposed to questioning along structured lines; the varieties of emphasis placed upon bio-medical or upon social components in the patients' history and problems; value assumptions used in diagnosis and treatment for different age, sex, class groups, and types of problems; feedback to patients and the degree to which this indicates consultation as a participative or expert approach. Such concerns are indicative of the sociologist's interpretation of medical practice as a social interaction, influenced by the characteristics of both doctors and patients, of prevailing social values as well as the application of medical/scientific knowledge to illness conditions. Blaxter (1978) in discussing diagnosis (and this could equally well be applied to treatment and rehabilitation) distinguishes between diagnosis-as-a-category, referring to a list of diseases, and diagnosis-as-a-process, referring the thing the physician does. Another set of concerns centres around the management of uncertainty in the face of illness: the relationship between patients' perception of their illness and its implications for recovery and the doctor's expert, and perhaps unrevealed, diagnosis and prognosis, the unfolding sequence of expectation, speculation and adaptation; and the differing approaches of physicians to the problems of their own uncertainties (McIntosh, 1977; Roth, 1963; Davis, 1960, 1963; Fox, 1957, 1959; Voysey, 1975). The nature of the patient's condition and the doctor's task impose themselves differentially upon the nature of patient-doctor interaction and sociologists have explored how the practice of surgery, obstetrics, paediatrics, psychiatry, or general practice each produce a specific form of inter-action and assumption of roles. Surgical consultation and procedures typically display perhaps most sharply the situation of the doctor as expert and the patient as a relatively naive and passive participant. In psychiatry, by comparison, the need for communication, exchange, and co-operation, and the element of counselling and advice, may heighten the degree of patient involvement and participation in both diagnosis and treatment whilst the doctor appears more as an orchestrator of the patient's own feelings and understandings about his problem. Davies (1979) for example shows how prevalent approaches to the treatment of alcoholism require the patient himself to define and accept his drinking problem, to achieve insight into his behaviour and its implications as a necessary pre-condition to a form of treatment which is essentially self-treatment. He also describes how this frequently causes puzzlement in patients whose previous experience of other illnesses has led them to expect other, more active types of medical intervention. In obstetrics and gynaecology, on the other hand, where the patient is frequently not ill, but experiencing a normal physiological process, recent developments have suggested resentment by patients at the over-technical management of events which have a deep emotional significance for them as women (Oakley, 1979, 1980).

Sociologists have also been interested in the effect on inter-action of the physical setting and associated social structures in which consultation and treatment take place. Hospital wards and clinics have their own social structure involving routines, specialization of tasks, and co-ordination of procedures and staff roles which have evolved for the management of business on a large and continuous scale and into which the patient must accommodate. Within such settings, however, a patient structure may emerge in which patients observe medical actions, exchange information about diagnoses and prognoses, and build up in-formally interpretations of what is happening to themselves and others (Fox, 1959; Roth, 1963; Davis, 1963; McIntosh, 1977; Glaser and Strauss, 1965). General practice as a setting for doctor-patient inter-action has received particular attention because of the variety of tasks involved in primary medical care, its strategic position in the process of referral and the diversity of its organiza-tional forms and of practitioners' definition of their roles. In studies of urban and rural practice in Northern Scotland and the Western Isles, Horobin and McIntosh (1977; Horobin, forth-coming) talked with practitioners about how, from the almost infinite number of tasks which they might perform and the roles they might play, they 'constructed' their job—how for example they determined priorities and balanced their various roles as medical experts, referral agents, family doctors, and community counsellors. The range of possibilities is conveyed in a few excerpts from the doctors' own statements:

Dr Smith: 'You see, to me, a doctor is a scientist. He should try his best to be a scientist all through and only then can he do justice to his profession. However sympathetic or kind one wants to be towards a family, he can't be a social worker. If I am a social worker, I am doing an injustice to my profession.'

Dr Bothwell: 'Because we're so overburdened by relative trivia and social problems, we cannot use the skills for which we're trained . . . we are trained to treat medical problems. . . . I would think that 30 to 40 per cent of my time is spent on what I've been trained for. The bulk of the rest of the work could be done by health visitors, social workers, district nurses—who are much cheaper and who are even trained for the job.'

The majority of practitioners proffered a very different interpretation.

Dr Richards: 'There's much more than medicine in it . . . we're not general practitioners, we're family doctors, which means you're a family friend.'

Dr Jackson: '[These problems] are not non-medical: they're part of life and really that's what we're dealing with.'

Dr McKenzie: 'People come here for a reason and I am prepared to deal with anything.'

Not surprisingly such different interpretations produced differing referral habits and job priorities. The reasons for such diversity are not yet clear. Isolated rural settings distant from major medical centres enforce self-reliance. Some doctors, however, had sought such settings just because lack of time-constraints and the close network of rural life afforded opportunities for family doctoring not available in large urban practices. In such instances it was the individual style of practitioners therefore rather than the physical and social setting which produced different job prescriptions. Self-selection may equally be involved in the choice of solo, dual, or group practice or participation in health centres and we are as yet only opening-up the relationship of individual preferences, organizational forms, and social settings to styles of doctoring. Doctors' retrospective accounts of what they do and why they do it, valuable in themselves, provide only one perspective on reality. Patients' accounts, as Stimson and Webb (1975) have shown, frequently yield different versions of the same event. Byrne and Long (1976), starting with a concern for medical education and its appropriateness for the problems encountered in general practice, provided unique material in an analysis of 2500 tape-recorded interviews. It is indicative of the relevance of research on medical work to medicine itself that this pioneering work was largely initiated and conducted by general practitioners. Such work may be intrinsically interesting to sociological students of social structure or of occupations, but well-documented research of how medicine is conducted by its varied practitioners in many clinical fields, in different settings and under various constraints of time and resources, seems a necessary foundation for medical education.

5

The health system

The British National Health Service, as an effective and civilized system for meeting the health needs of the population, requires no elaborate justification or defence. The broad objectives of the Service were distilled by the Royal Commission on the National Health Service into seven principles.

> We believe that the NHS should:
>   encourage and assist individuals to remain healthy
>   provide equality of entitlement to health services
>   provide a broad range of services of a high standard
>   provide equality of access to these services
>   provide a service free at the time of use
>   satisfy the reasonable expectations of its users
>   remain a national service responsible to local needs.

These are comprehensive principles embodying a high standard of political morality. My own remarks spring from a strong appreciation of the general principles of the Service and I welcome the Commission's favourable verdict. But if the principles of the NHS need no defence compared with those of other health systems, it needs critical review of a more fundamental kind than it received from the Royal Commission.

Until recently British sociologists heavily pre-occupied with professionalism and with doctor–patient interaction in a host of specific settings and services have tended to study the parts more assiduously than the whole. Findings from specific studies can, however, be partially synthesized and can be supplemented by more direct work carried out by sociologists (e.g. Atkinson et al, 1979; Blaxter, 1976; Davis, 1979; Hart, 1978; Stacey, 1976; Stacey et al, 1976), by students of administration and social policy (e.g. Bayley, 1973; Brown, 1979; Forsyth, 1973; Hunter, 1980; Klein, 1973, 1975, 1976; Kogan et al, 1978; Moroney 1976), by economists (e.g. Cooper, 1975; Culyer, 1973, 1976; Culyer and

Wright, 1978; Hauser, 1972; Mooney, Russell and Weir, 1980), socially-minded physicians (e.g. Cochrane, 1972; Hart, 1971; McKeown, 1976; Owen, 1976; Powles, 1973), and by sociologists from overseas and particularly from the USA (e.g. McKinlay, 1979; Mechanic, 1971, 1974; Rein, 1976; Walters, 1980). Reading this diverse literature I have been struck by constant repetitions of the same themes and conclusions. It seems that there are certain *self-evident truths*, not perhaps held by all sociological students of the NHS, nor by any means confined to sociologists. This chapter is devoted to their exposition.

A. THE NATURE OF HEALTH AND MEDICINE

1. *Health and illness are social concepts*

At the extremes of physical robustness and well being and of crippling and painful disease or madness there may be near universal agreements about who is well or ill and what constitutes health and illness. Between these extreme states judgement is conditional upon:

the age, sex, family status, occupation, class position, and geographical and temporal location of the person;

the activity of the individual, his interaction with, relationship to, and dependence upon others;

the frequency of the illness condition, the responsibility of the individual for the onset of the condition, the existence of remedies, the availability of treatment services, the patterns of illness in the society, and the position of the condition in the general spectrum of illnesses defined in terms of trivia, seriousness, pain, curability, and cost;

the orientation of the individual towards the recognition, acceptance, resistance or denial of symptoms, and the relationship of the observer to the affected individual and the professional affiliation of the observer.

The literature abounds with examples of conditions classed as illness or non-illnesses in different societies and levels of technology and, within our own society, of unrecognized and untreated conditions equivalent in numbers and severity to those being treated. The phenomenon of the 'clinical iceberg' (Last, 1963) is well known and is probably best illustrated in the epidemiological survey conducted by Wadsworth et al (1971) in two London boroughs. In a randomly selected sample of 1000 persons monitored over a two week period they found that almost all (951) reported at least one symptom or illness condition. Of these, 188 took no action of any kind, 562 took non-medical action (e.g. resting or change in diet), 168 consulted their GPs, 28 attended an out-patient clinic, and 5 were admitted to hospital. These findings confirm other estimates of total morbidity and, more important for our purposes, they underline the need for self-reports in any attempt to define health and illness.

The ordinary respondent has only a rudimentary knowledge of anatomy and physiology but certain types of 'data' are available to him which are normally inaccessible to the doctor. This is particularly true in relation to the increasingly used global self-estimate in which the respondent is asked to assess his overall health. Little is known about the cognitive and motivational factors underlying answers to such a question but it seems that the respondent draws on a wide range of data; comparisons between his present and past health, his own health in relation to other people of his age, his health in relation to his life-style and his hopes and expectations for the future. Rather than measuring something less than 'objective' clinical assessments, self-reports may be measuring something more. The basis for this claim lies firstly, in the wide range of objective and subjective realities which the respondent draws on, secondly, in the assumption that the most important reality for him is his own definition of the situation, and thirdly, in the assumption that his attitudes and behaviour will depend on how he defines himself. These assumptions are borne out in a number of studies which show that a respondent's perception of his own health has more effect on his health related behaviour than his 'objective' health, as assessed by medical examination (Taylor 1979).

2. *Differential morbidity and mortality are largely attributable to differences in social experience*
This statement, referring not to subjectively or socially-defined

illness, but to medically diagnosable conditions, has its basis in repeated observations and vital statistical analyses. Differentials have been most fully documented in relation to Social Class. The *Decennial Supplement for England and Wales 1970–2* (Registrar General, 1978) estimated that

a new-born male subject from birth to age 64 to the Social Class I (mortality) rates and then at subsequent ages to rates 20 per cent lower than the national rates would expect to live 7·17 years longer than one subject to the equivalent rates for Social Class V and then rates 20 per cent higher than the national rates.

The significance of an increased life-expectancy of 7·17 years is put in perspective by the fact that between 1950 and 1977 the average life expectancy of males at age 1 year increased by only 3·4 years. It should be further borne in mind that all other classes, containing the bulk of the population, also have lower life expectancies than Social Class I. There is general agreement too that these differences reflect

(1) poorer growth and physical development in childhood and adolescence which will influence susceptibility to disease throughout later years;

(2) greater exposure to life- and health-threatening environmental conditions and behavioural styles;

(3) unequal use of preventive measures and of health services;

(4) unequal access to the best standards of medical care.

Data on morbidity, though less reliable, point in the same direction.

Differences in social experience however are not confined to differential class position. Considerable evidence has accumulated to show the poorer living standards, increased vulnerability, and unequal medical and social care of specific sub-groups of the population, the mentally retarded, the mentally ill, the physically handicapped, the long-term chronic sick, the unemployed, the elderly, the members of one-parent families, and young working-class mothers. Whilst diverse in their social situations, such groups tend to share certain characteristics—lack of economic productivity and power, behaviour at variance with accepted norms, problems of multiple aetiology, and the low susceptibility of their problems to the curative techniques carrying most prestige in the professional world.

A further class of health problems created by social action or inaction stems from collective arrangements for the provision of food, shelter, transport, and work. They have already been comprehensively identified by McKeown and there is little dissent in principle from the need for preventive control of environmental pollution, road safety hazards, and the consumption of drugs, tobacco, and unhealthy foods. Opposition to such control is often justified by reference to the freedom of choice of the individuals but, in practice, these hazards are differentially distributed across regions, classes and age-groups, and their deliberate retention could alternatively be defined as a violation of their freedom.

3. Medical definitions of health are disease-centred and do not provide an adequate basis for social policy and action

Medical reactions against the sociologists' use of the term 'medical model' are often sharp and angry. At times, when the term is loosely used or ill-understood the reaction is justified. It is not, however, in its best usage, an accusation of inhumanity or a personal indictment directed at the practices of individual practitioners. It contains an implicit set of definitions of the health needs of modern societies (see chapter 4), an analysis of the fundamental principles of medical science, education, and organization, and a judgement that these principles are an insufficient basis for the development of health policy and practice.

There are several threads to the argument. First, there is the empirical argument that systems of lay thought and action already exist, sometimes with complex formulations of the causes of illness and disease, of appropriate treatments and of relevant behavioural responses. They may differ from medical thought and action and can frequently be shown to be factually inaccurate, but even where lay and medical formulations about cause and treatment coincide they may well have different subjective meanings and different implications for action. Many of the symptoms and problems brought to the medical practitioner may be defined by the practitioner as non-medical and not susceptible to medical skills, but may constitute health problems in the definition of lay persons, of social therapists or of the World Health Organization.

The second strand of the argument is that medical education is disease-oriented, that it deals with patients not persons and situations, that it is primarily practised in clinics and hospitals and that treatment is typically directed at the individual rather than his problem. his social circumstances and behaviour. Moreover medical organization is such that whenever treatment and action is educational, developmental, environmental, preventive, or supportive it tends to be marginal to medical science and practice, and the services which cater primarily for these needs within medicine lack both prestige and resources.

The third strand of argument contends that, although medical science has reduced the threat of severe illness to survival, it has released or created new needs, for care, counselling, and rehabilitation which require modes of diagnosis and treatment for which medicine is educationally, professionally, and organizationally not equipped, but over which it continues to exercise administrative responsibility and power. It has also extended its responsibility to a range of behavioural problems (e.g. alcohol and drug abuse, development problems, deviant behaviour, and disturbance of social relationships) to which it applies the palliative methods of individualistic medicine and thus treats symptoms rather than cause. Whilst the argument may have force when applied to the whole profession it cannot be pushed too far without encountering contrary evidence from the best practices of family doctors, psychiatrists, obstetricians, paediatricians, and geriatricians.

These are not arguments against medicine. As I noted earlier, many sociologists, particularly in the radical fervour of the 1960s and early 1970s, complained that medicine had already overstepped its disciplinary boundary and was in danger of medicalizing everything. In retrospect this latter indictment of medicine may have been a particular manifestation of widespread protest against specialization and the bureaucratization of everyday life and the tendency to sub-divide, in terms acceptable to particular professions and skills, objective and subjective states which, to the individual, are inter-connected and indivisible.

B. CHARACTER OF MODERN HEALTH SYSTEMS

Some of the characteristics of our present health systems on which I identify widespread agreement are implicit in the above remarks about the nature of health and merely require re-statement rather than explanation. They are:

4. The health system is disease-oriented and hospital-centred

5. The operation of the health system has had little impact on long-standing inequality or on life expectations

Other characteristics, whilst previously mentioned, do require further elaboration.

6. Prevention, in which the scope for reduction of disease and death is potentially much greater than intervention at the point of illness, is under-emphasized, fragmentary, and frequently contradictory

Even the terminology in this field is unsatisfactory. 'Positive health' is a shadowy concept, difficult for many people to grasp. 'Preventive health care' seems to carry an internal contradiction. 'Disease-prevention' emphasizes a negative, defensive approach and 'health-promotion' smacks of progaganda. Anthropologists would probably say that the absence of words for a concept signifies the absence of the concept in that culture. Whilst that is not entirely true of positive health, the vastly different weights given to the treatment of disease and the promotion of health give it a relative truth.

Assessing the economic costs and benefits and the relative feasibility of preventive health care, Warner (1979) distinguishes three sets of measures, those delivered by individuals to individuals (e.g. immunization, anti-smoking counselling, pap smears, and check-ups) by the community to individuals (e.g. family planning or anti-smoking campaigns through the media) and by the community to the community (e.g. fluoridation, and anti-pollution legislation).

The individual-to-individual approach is simultaneously the most flexible and the most erratic of the three measures depending, as it does, upon the knowledge and motivation of members of the public, the frequency and purpose of their contact with health personnel, and the acceptance by the professional that counselling and prevention are an integral part of his responsibilities. The approach has worked reasonably well, if with some hiccups, in relation to the immunization of children, but it is significant that in this instance the individual approach has been supplemented and reinforced by governmental backing. For decades it hardly worked at all in relation to family planning because lack of a positive planning orientation by large sections of the public coincided with reluctance or opposition of doctors to accept active responsibility for counselling, the provision of contraceptives, the termination of pregnancy, or the reduction of risk through sterilization or vasectomy. Check-ups and screening procedures, which come nearest to using medical expertise, are highly variable in their coverage, effectiveness, and efficiency. There is widespread agreement that the individual approach has been least effective in the field of preventive dentistry. Given the ambivalence of the public towards preventive health care and the distance and uncertainty of the future rewards, the individual-to-individual approach is only likely to yield substantial results in specific fields such as family planning where new socio-economic pressures on the individual create strong public (and particularly middle-class) demand, where the doctor is directly rewarded for his preventive activities, and where governmental policy provides multi-faceted support for both patients and the professions.

One purpose of the community-to-individual approach is to create motivations which have not hitherto existed and thus to provide clientele for the individual-to-individual approach. There is widespread scepticism about its most characteristic vehicle, health education. In part this reflects the moral/political dilemma of governments intervening to influence public values and the attitudes and behaviour of individuals in intimate matters. In a pluralist society without a clearly articulated set of principles about the relationship of public good to individual liberty, this is a common dilemma. Perhaps the DHSS dictum that health is everybody's business is best interpreted as a gentle shot in that direction. Another source of scepticism stems from doubt about the efficacy of health education and media campaigns. The specific contribution of educational and propaganda campaigns is inherently difficult to evaluate in a context of general social change and cross-currents of thought. With flexible evaluative techniques (see chapter 6) and a firm public policy backed up by research funds, it is by no means impossible. More difficult, and urgently requiring fundamental research, is knowledge about how to change public attitudes and individual behaviour. Do we know enough about the dynamics of public policy, public opinion, 'educational' input, individual values, and the triggers of behavioural change? What is the impact of knowledge upon individual behaviour compared with economic incentives, social disapproval, and other felt pressures? What are the major cancelling-out effects of contrary propaganda and of contradictions in public policy?

Contradictions can and do frequently exist between community-to-individual measures and community-to-community measures. Evidence of long-term ambivalence about the fluoridation of water supplies is paralleled by governmental reluctance to legislate or enforce legislation on drunken driving, speed limits, vehicle safety, use of car seat-belts, and air and river pollution, or even to maintain by taxation the cost of tobacco and alcohol. *Pace* health educationalists, environmental health officers, and a few weakly-supported organizations, it could be argued that 'prevention is nobody's business'. It is perhaps nostalgic to regret the passing of the Medical Officer of Health and the submergence and invisibility of 'community health specialists' within the hospital- and disease-oriented health service, but visibility, independence and conflict may be essential for the correction of institutionalized imbalance.

7. The health system is slow to respond to new demographic and social needs

Examples of the slow responsiveness of the health system to social change have occurred throughout the preceding pages—the long-drawn-out and reluctant adjustment to birth control, sterilization and abortion, the failure to deal with regional and class inequality, the retention of a disease-centred organizational framework, the emphasis upon bio-medical research in the face of major health service problems and research requirements, and the low value still placed upon prevention. Other examples recur frequently in the literature but our final judgement must clearly be a comparative one. Compared with the non-adaptation of UK industry and the archaic irrelevance of some features of our universities, of our legal system or of British Trade Union thought, the efficiency and effectiveness of our health system could well be admired. Change in any complex bureaucratic institution in the face of ambivalent governmental policy, the wide spectrum of public opinion and the history, training, and interests of its work-force is inherently difficult. Brown's (1979) question about the 1974 reorganization of the NHS (*New Bottles: Old Wine?*) obviously has a much wider applicability. Current complaints about slow responsiveness relate primarily to what have been called 'the Cinderella services', the services for the mentally and physically handicapped, the mentally ill, the chronic sick, and the elderly. The essential problem is the slow pace of diverting emphasis and resources towards these populations, and of creating comprehensive and effective services for their care. The sources of the problem lie in demographic change, the longer survival (partially due to past medical advances) of vulnerable categories of the population, increased social and physical mobility, the greater involvement of women in the workforce, and perhaps a heightened public moral sensitivity towards deprived and disabled persons. Resistance to change is generally associated with the medical model, its incorporation into service structures and the profession's concept of its role and in the differential power bases of the established and emerging interests. The problem is compounded by an over-bureaucratized management system, by shortage of sufficient new monies to effect significant painless shifts, and by the administrative and professional separation of the health and the social services.

The situation was well summarized by Blaxter (1979) in an Appendix to the Royal Commission on the NHS on a different but related question, that of rehabilitation of the disabled:

It could well be suggested that the strongest criticism which could be levelled at our society's provisions for the rehabilitation and welfare of disabled people is that they are highly hypocritical. There is considerable agreement about the general principles which ought to be applied, but action in every area of health and welfare is confined to cosmetic tinkering with the system, adding new details here and exhortations there but avoiding at all costs any fundamental change which will upset the balance of existing systems.

She concluded:

The field of disability and rehabilitation has been characterized, during the last 20 or 30 years, by a multiplicity of official reports of high quality. The need is not so much for the establishment of new principles, which are now quite generally agreed, but for the sweeping away of old structures which impede the implementation of these policies.

8. Gross variations in the allocation of resources and in their utilization indicate the need for firmer criteria and quality control

Evidence under this heading refers to several different areas of health service operation:

(a) Variations in the allocation of resources to different regions which bear no obvious relationship to medically-defined needs. Following the implementation of the proposals of the Resource Allocation Working Party (DHSS, 1976) for England and similar bodies for Wales and Scotland, there is reason to believe that, over time, the grosser anomalies will be phased out. Doubts remain, however, about the validity of the health indicators to be used in reallocation and about the political and moral basis of a 'fair shares' distribution, and particularly the degree to which reallocation of health resources should be used to correct inequalities in health whose origin lies in inter-regional inequalities in general economic prosperity.

(b) Variations in the allocation of resources to different types of service. Two separate arguments are used. First, it is widely noted that, in terms of provision of resources in relation to estimates of 'need', certain sectors, particularly those relating to mental illness, mental retardation, the elderly, and the chronic sick, are consistently under-financed. Secondly, within this overall distribution, there are marked disparities between regions and areas in the number of doctors, other health personnel, beds, waiting times, and costs per in-patient week.

(c) The criteria used for different types of treatment and care vary between regions and areas, between hospitals and between consultants. The most-quoted instances refer to surgical operations such as tonsillectomy and appendicectomy and more recently cholecystectomy (Fowkes, 1980) where it is widely believed that variations bear little relationship to morbidity or to agreed diagnostic criteria but reflect the availability of surgeon-time and of beds and the idiosyncratic practices of particular consultants. Surgical variations, however, probably receive prominence because they are easily measureable. Studies of general practice show equally wide variations in consultation rates per patient and in the proportion of doctors' time spent on various patient groups. The frequent implication from writers as different as Illich and Cochrane (neither of whom would wish to be classed as sociologists) is that many operative interventions are unnecessary and undesirable.

Several important caveats are necessary. Some variations reflect deliberate, carefully-considered policy rather than happenstance, e.g. the more cautious approach in Scotland to the de-institutionalization of patients in mental hospitals. Others reflect a policy emphasizing a different mix of services, low provision for one kind of care being compensated by other measures. Within small areas the true position is often concealed by cross-border flows. Perhaps the most important caveat is the comparative one made by McPherson et al (1980) in an analysis of the incidence of eight common surgical operations between and within Canada, the USA and the UK. Whilst large variations occurred within the UK, which were partially attributable to supply variables and referral and decision procedures, the most striking results are the much lower operation rates in the UK compared with either Canada or the USA and the much weaker correlation in the UK between operation rates and surgical manpower. They conclude:

What can certainly be said, however, is that the National Health Service is a good deal cheaper than many others and, given the great uncertainty surrounding the indications for most of these procedures, its outcomes are not manifestly worse than those of the other two systems studied here.

9. The health system in its policy formation, its management and operation is professionally dominated and methods of both internal and external control are weak

Sociologists start from the background assumption that the health system is a public social service carried out by skilled manpower, organized through Health Departments, Health Authorities, and ultimately accountable to the public. Countries differ sharply in the structure of their health services, in the financing of health care, in the location of policy-making power and the mechanisms by which public need is translated into demand and supply, but the importance of health care has impelled all developed societies to establish procedures for the development of policies, the allocation of responsibilities and the regulation of work. British arrangements differ from those of other capitalist countries in exercising more governmental control over policy, budgets and their use, but the fundamental principle that the health system is subject to a degree of public control is acknowledged in all developed societies. Nor is there any fundamental difference between the provision of health care and of other social services. There are, however, major differences between social services in their degree of internal and external control which stem from historical influences, the nature of the service being supplied, the populations to which it is offered, the training and organization of the workers, and the availability of alternative services. Some of the observations especially relevant to questions of control and accountability in the health system are:

that, of all the major services, only the health service is not directly administered by elected representatives at national or local government level;

that the sources of power and decision-making are diffuse and that in consequence accountability is weak;

that the standards of individual and service care and competence vary widely;

that the dominant profession in the health system claims clinical autonomy in its treatment of patients and will not accept external supervision and regulation;

that, in the absence of external control, strong opposition has
prevented the development of effective methods of collegial
control and audit;

that the machinery for the judgement of complaints and the
disciplining of doctors is dominated by doctors;

that national policies are difficult to implement if they are contrary to the balance of existing medical opinion and interests;

that, in the absence of regulatory mechanisms, decisions taken
at clinical level and defended by the principle of clinical
autonomy create costs and de facto policies which impede
planning and financial control;

that effectiveness and efficiency are weakened because treatments and services are not strictly evaluated;

that because of professionally-dominated consensus management and consultative procedures, the policy-making role
of Health Boards and their members is very limited;

that, because the non-elected local health councils were granted
restricted powers, access and responsibilities there is little
scope for the public to participate in the formulation and
implementation of policy.

Similar charge sheets could be drawn up for almost any public
sector service and they could perhaps be defended with less ease.
Sociologists have wisely not yet applied the same procedure to
their University Departments or to their Universities, where
clinical freedom is paralleled by academic freedom—and where
every item on the above list would have its equivalent. Social
workers, brought up in the shadow of medicine, whilst administered by elected local authorities, are developing a similarly
strong professional authority and discretionary power. Sociological
observations on the nature of power, decision-making and
accountability in health systems are an expression of the dilemma
arising in all publicly-provided services delivered through
bureaucratized machinery by professionally organized groups.
The dilemma is that of ensuring an effective and efficient service,
delivered evenly according to agreed principles, and at the same
time to facilitate that degree of flexibility, judgement, and discretion which variations between individuals, groups, and
regions requires, and which will engage the motivation of highly-

skilled workers. Freidson (1975) in a study in the USA of a 'model medical group deliberately set up to be as close as possible to the ideal of liberal medical reformers' which during the course of his study included, for some period of time, more than 50 full- or part-time physicians responsible for about 25,000 enrolled patients, encountered problems of clinical autonomy, quality control and accountability essentially similar to those listed above. He concluded:

I suggest that no formal method of organizing the financing and presentation of health care can solve these problems because, by their nature, formal methods either destroy the possibility for sustaining 'sensitive personal relationships' (as is the case in automation or industrialisation) or allow discretion without being able to control how it is exercised (as is the case in virtually all present policy schemes in the United States). Formal methods of control rely on formal modes of accounting, underneath which can flourish a variety of stances and relationships.

What, then, can be done? Certainly no solution lies in a return to the traditional system of a nominally free market of services within a medical monopoly. Formal planning of administrative controls over the financing, distribution and accountability of health service remains necessary and desirable. Also necessary and desirable are a variety of devices designed to provide formal assurance of greater consumer influence on policy-making and day-to-day operation of health care organisations. Both modes of control are likely to improve the *form* of health service. The *spirit* of service, however, can be improved only by changes in those aspects of the everyday milieu of health care which mobilise, activate and guide the health workers' own unique capacities to exercise collective discipline over their discretionary work . . . collective participation in governing that work is as essential as performing it. It is only a technician who defines his job as simply doing his work. A self-governing worker must consider it to be part of his work to attend to the work of his colleagues while keeping his own work visible to them. Thus deliberate mutual observation and evaluation of performance must be a legitimate part of responsible etiquette, as must be the obligation to discuss one's observations and evaluations with others.

Unfortunately Freidson declined to provide the blueprint of such a system.

C. POLICY PLANNING AND IMPLEMENTATION

10. Health policy is obscure in its origins and weak in its application

Sociologists have received enough encouragement and enough access from enough clinicians to have built up a detailed picture of the ideology and practice of medicine and the operation of health services. They are encouraged by the Health Departments to undertake health services research. I am aware of very few instances where sociologists from outside the Departments have been encouraged or given access to carry out research, for publication, on the policy process at national level. Perhaps that is why sociologists, who have no employment base within the service, feel that the origins of policy are obscure. By using the increasing volume of official statistics, sociologists and other students of policy can trace trends, outcomes, variations and anomalies in the application of policy, but as I shall argue in chapter 6, evaluation of policy and of complex services requires more than the formal methodology appropriate for clinical trials. Sociologists are wont to state that in these fields 'outcome is process', by which they mean that links exist in a chain of events beginning with the identification of problems, the formulation and re-formulation of objectives, the quality and validity of the information base used in policy discussion, the development and choice of alternative strategies, and the measures used to implement strategies as well as documentation of outcomes. At each stage definitions are made, criteria adopted, constraints experienced and options rejected, each of which affects priorities, objectives, and implementation. These are not merely management decisions, they contain explicit or implicit judgements about social need and result from negotiation between individuals and groups representing particular interests. Studies of the policy process would initially reveal the inadequacies and conflict which occur in policy formulation and implementation in any public or private sector organization, but, in the long run, I believe they also produce clarification and understanding. This is a major area of sociological (indeed social science) research urgently needing development. The case studies

97

conducted at break-neck speed by Professor Kogan and his team (1978) at the request of the Royal Commission on the NHS indicate the potentiality of such research.

General agreement about the slow pace of policy change and the progressive reduction in its impact as it moves down to field level is accompanied by recognition of the inevitable difficulties of accomplishing change in any large-scale nationally-administered service with a decentralized structure. Freidson's general comments on the problems of reconciling quality control with the discretionary judgements of motivated professionals are pertinent to this issue. Several commentators (Brown, 1979; Klein, 1976a) have called attention to the syndicalist nature of the reorganized structure. Klein points out that in the past syndicalism or workers' control in the NHS has been largely confined to general practitioners and hospital consultants and has applied mainly to their powers of decision-making at the point of delivery. The reorganized structure extends the practice to other professions and categories of workers both at Board level, in consensus management, and in advisory arrangements. Elsewhere (1976b) discussing the time-constraints on policy change he quotes a DHSS circular listing the bodies whose comments should be sought before an area health authority may close or change the use of a health building.

These are: community health councils, local authorities, joint staff consultative committees, family practitioner committees, appropriate local advisory committees (including the statutory medical advisory committee for the area concerned), local medical committees, and 'any other body or person not covered by the above which the AHA considers should be consulted—for example, voluntary organisations.'

Apart from the practical impact of syndicalism and consultation upon policy change and implementation, sociological interest centres upon two related issues, conflict of interests and objectives, and the potential effect of structure upon behaviour.

The concept of social order, how it is maintained, and how deviance is controlled, has always been a central issue in sociology. One strand of sociological thought, based heavily on Marxist theory, sees conflict as an integral feature of social life in capitalist societies stemming from unequal wealth and power in production, distribution, and exchange. The perspective is undoubtedly pertinent to change within the NHS, not only because of the unequal rewards for different categories of workers, but also because, in a no-growth budget, change inevitably involves the withdrawal of funds from some individuals and (organized) groups of workers and its redistribution to others. This affects rewards, autonomy, and relative power. Conflict of interests in this sense means conflict of career and money interests. More recent sociological theory, originally derived from philosophical thought, but now resting on firm empirical evidence, sees conflict as inevitable not because of class divisions but because the differential experience and situation of individuals in all social organizations leads them to different perceptions and interpretations of the 'real world'. In NHS terms the real worlds of health and illness and consequently the desired objectives and priorities discerned by community nurses, general practitioners, and medical specialists, by administrative medical officers, hospital porters and pharmacists. and by the staff of sheltered houses, old people's homes, and mental hospitals look very different. These viewpoints are reinforced and organized by loyalty-creating training institutions and workers' associations. This conflict of interests is perceptual, cognitive, and emotional and only partially related to the other category.

Both sources of conflict are relevant to the question of how far and in what ways organizational structures affect occupational behaviour. The issue is complex. Many well-documented instances exist where, for example, the physical or administrative sub-division of an organization leads to decline in communication, the bureaucratization of decisions and the drifting apart of objectives. The separation of the health and social services undoubtedly leads to barriers in planning and practice but after studying the jointly administered health and social services of Northern Ireland Kogan (1978) concluded:

Where work is highly technical and specialist, or is based on particular philosophies, as is true of the whole range of health and welfare services, working together may not be easily secured by the simple application of solutions such as co-terminosity or organisational integration.

On the intended integration of general practitioners into the main stream of the NHS, he noted the relative ineffectiveness of structural change in the face of the independent contractual status so highly prized by doctors and commented:

The motives and incentives for change lie elsewhere than in organisational change. No clear recommendation on this issue can be made therefore, which does not include a radical change of concepts and values. . . .

And more generally he concluded: 'Changes in structure do not necessarily affect behaviour if there is no motivated inducement.'

The detailed knowledge necessary for the development of data-based theory and its application is limited and frequently impressionistic—partly because of restricted opportunities for first-hand study. Sociologists, however, have built up a body of material on medical and other professional work and are increasingly interested in health and the division of labour (Stacey et al, 1977).

Economists are beginning to work on programme budgeting, unit budgets and resource management (Perrin et al, 1978) and health economics is being built up alongside medical sociology as a social science resource (Culyer, 1976; Culyer and Wright, 1978; Mooney et al, 1980; Williams and Anderson, 1975). There is much to be done before we embark on further structural change designed to achieve firmer policy implementation. It would help that work considerably if the policy process were as open to research and observation as clinical practice has become.

11. The separation of health and social services is a barrier to comprehensive policy, planning, and practice
This is not the preface to a plea for further structural integration but a re-statement of empirical observations and a reflection on the consequences of the division of labour in societies of high technology. Specialization has brought benefits in technical advances and in expert care which in many fields of science, industry, and in personal social services could probably not have been achieved in other ways. But when the total needs of patients and clients have been broken down into their constituent parts and each part allocated to workers who have the skills, resources,

and facilities to deal expertly with each part, the parts have to be put together again to achieve the original objective of meeting the individual's needs. The process of breaking-down needs and providing expert specialized skills eventually reaches the point at which the process itself creates its own needs. In a mass-production industry volume production alienates workers whose minute and mechanized contribution produces no reward other than monetary compensation for daily drudgery. In the professional/personal services field drudgery of specialized tasks has been avoided by granting to each specialty a high degree of autonomy in making decisions about the objectives of their speciality, the organization of professional education and of their service and in defining the needs of their clients. The welfare of their clients thus becomes synonymous with the welfare of the profession and the services it wishes to develop and extend.

The 'solutions' of (professionally-dominated) policy in the 1970s were the internal integration of each major service and the establishment of co-ordinating machinery and cross-service collaboration (the equivalent at national level of the Nato-Comecon dialogue). But since each service is autonomous in its definition of the problem and its use of its own budget, collaboration is difficult to achieve. The position was summarized by investigators who had studied health service/local authority collaboration in four geographical areas. They described the clear belief of officers in these services that the need for collaboration should take place, instanced minor examples of the sharing of equipment and information, and concluded:

Beyond that the practical experience of collaboration ceases. Attempts to plan jointly the provision of services in pursuit of some common objective/goal relating to the health and welfare of the community have generally not been undertaken. And yet this should arguably be the ultimate aim of collaboration. The case for collaboration does not rest on matters such as avoiding the duplication of services (although such matters are of importance) but on the fact that both health and local authorities are in a general sense concerned with the well-being of the community, with the satisfaction of social and health needs—with social planning. It is at this level that conceptual and practical problems are immense. Social planning is characterised by (a) a low level of understanding of the relationship between means and ends; (b) a high level of disagreement over both means and ends; (c) extreme difficulty in establishing operational concepts of social needs; (d) a high level of disagreement between the contributing professions as to how needs should be met and the effectiveness of particular methods of treatment. (Norton and Rogers, 1977)

A rather similar diagnosis was presented by another investigator (Brown, 1979), who had studied the establishment and early work of the Humberside Area Health Authority:

But the development of a mental health service does not lie entirely with the health authority. Some of the most important elements, including sheltered housing, hostels and social support, are the responsibility of local social service departments. Here there is no equivalent of the community health council and seldom any political pressure to counteract those favouring services for children and the elderly, which come from the same budget. The main pressure group for the mentally ill, in fact, is the area health authority which wants to see local authority services develop in order to relieve its own. But it has little to offer in exchange, and its only weapons are persuasion (on the statutory joint planning machinery) and the power to contribute to the initial cost of relevant local authority projects.

Rather similar considerations apply to the other Cinderella services for the mentally handicapped and to a lesser extent the elderly. All suffer a double handicap because responsibility is divided and both sides have more attractive uses for their money. Many health experts believe that those services will never be planned effectively unless health authorities assume responsibility for social as well as medical care. This would entail a third stage in the removal of health and related services from local to central control (the first being the nationalisation of hospitals in 1948 and the second the absorption of local health authority services in 1974). It would be fiercely resisted on jurisdictional grounds by local authority interest groups. It would also entail dismantling the integrated social services departments which were created in 1971 on the implementation of the Seebohm Report and abandoning the rather dubious philosophy in that report about generic social workers. But that might cause more cheers than tears.

Considerable doubt has arisen about the possibilities of collaboration between separately administered authorities. This was expressed in a joint statement by a Director of Social Services and his local Area Medical Officer who felt that collaboration was more dependent on the attitudes and personality of the chief officers than on any structural arrangement. They said:

It seems remarkable that any collaboration can take place at all between the National Health Service and Local Government, since their two systems would appear to be totally incompatible. Furthermore, in our view, no co-operative machinery can alter the fact that there is a built-in tension between health and social services because, in a time of scarce resources and growing pressures, each is tempted to unload clients onto the other. For instance, hospitals for the mentally-handicapped are quite properly trying to discharge patients to reduce occupancy levels and so raise standards, which puts additional strains on local authority hostels and adult training centres, which are also under pressure to take people from the community. Equally, matrons of old people's homes are claiming that they are being required to take residents who should properly be placed in geriatric wards, while hospitals are wanting to discharge patients to old people's homes who are blocking beds, often in acute wards. The hospital authorities are concerned to speed up turnover of patients by earlier discharge and this makes further demands on the Home Help Service, which is already overstretched. Even if health and social services were under the same control, there would still be tensions on the allocation of resources as between the hospital and the community side of the services. (Stacey and Forsyth, 1976).

Similar findings about the problems of collaboration are reported by many investigators in other fields such as rehabilitation of the disabled (Keeble, 1979; Breverton and Daniel, 1971; Lee, 1975; Blaxter, 1976; Hyman, 1979), the care of the elderly (Skeet, 1974; National Corporation for the Care of Old People, 1979; Scammells, 1971), relationships between general practitioners and social workers (Reilly et al, 1977; Ratoff et al, 1974) and between medical social workers and their local authority colleagues (Johnson and Johnson, 1973, 1977).

The problem is not simply one of administrative responsibilities but is compounded by differing ideologies of need and treatment. Structural reorganization alone would not, therefore, produce a clear solution. Somewhere in the middle of the problem the self-perceived needs of clients have been replaced by professionals' conceptions of client's and of their own professional needs. The question for solution is therefore how to ensure that public and professional health should coincide.

D. FUTURE OF THE NHS

Reading the international literature and talking to colleagues abroad I am often struck by a simple paradox. I find that other advanced societies are pre-occupied with problems very similar in kind to those identified by policy-makers, professionals, and academics in the UK—the moral outlook and behaviour of children and young people, delinquency, sexual freedom, marital and family dissolution, abortion, the problems of inner cities, alcoholism, the care of the elderly and handicapped, industrial disputes, issues of pollution and conservation, the inexorable growth of bureaucracy—and the cost of health, the control of the health system, the high level of demand for health care, the need for community care policies, etc. They do, of course, differ in degree, both in the scale of the problem and in the efficacy of systems for dealing with them. What is remarkably paradoxical is the extent to which individuals and (particularly) the media in each country, see these problems as characteristic of their own society and of institutions and events peculiar to themselves. Those perceptions are, of course, the necessary precursors and motivators for reformist social action. They can, however, because of their ethnocentricity, be misleading indicators resulting in counterproductive measures. A more parsimonious explanation would suggest that advanced societies experience common problems because long term developments in technology and methods of production involving parallel developments in education, wealth and ways of life, in the relationships between individuals and groups in the family, industry and government create similar pressures. Differences in cultural traditions and institutions and in collective arrangements for the production and distribution of wealth, the welfare of individuals and groups and regulation of relationships through governmental intervention will mean that the manifestations of change differ from country to country. Appropriate action needs to take account of the underlying trends and pressures as well as their particular manifestations. Wholesale restructuring of an institution or organization because it is seen as the source of a national problem when other societies are experiencing the same problem despite their different organizational arrangements can bring unnecessary disruption.

From this point of view the re-affirmaton of the NHS by the recent Royal Commission and its restriction to nuts-and-bolts reform was undoubtedly wise. The concerns which had led to the structural reorganization of 1974, and to the establishment of the Commission, the unease felt by so many segments of the workforce, the disillusionment with reorganization, the disappointment at the Commission's slow-reform approach are themselves indications that adaptation is taking place albeit in an economic climate that prohibts the easy option of change through growth.

The 'self-evident truths' that I have distilled from constant repetition and consensus in the sociologically-oriented literature need supplementation by other general observations before the future of the NHS is considered. The earlier idea that the demand for health care would wither away under the impact of a comprehensive free health service is now as untenable as Lenin's doctrine that the State would wither away in a truly communist society. Health comes to mean something different, less focused on biological states and nearer to what Herzlich's respondents called 'equilibrium' and which I translate as 'well-being'. To the attainment of well-being there is no end and, since resources are finite, rationing is inevitable. The fee-for-service approach, whilst it might result in a larger proportion of GNP being devoted to health, and particularly to disease, is irrelevant to this larger problem and if applied on any scale would reinforce many of the imbalances, inequities, and historical hang-overs discussed above. The use of economic criteria for the distribution of resources within a free service is an entirely different matter.

Four questions are at issue:

Whose priorities?
How are they to be determined?
How can they be implemented?
How can they be evaluated?

The choice is between different modes of intervention and the philosophies on which they are based. They can be presented in dichotomies as follows:
between

medical definitions	or	social definitions of health
medical intervention	or	ameliorative social action
personal service	or	collective/environmental measures
disease-treatment	or	health promotion
institutionalized care	or	effective community care

Each dichotomy has implications for different target populations; children, young adults and the elderly; the temporarily, minimally, acutely, and chronically sick; patients and non-patients; today's and tomorrow's populations. In practice we are not faced by mutually exclusive dichotomies but by questions of balance and of emphasis. We cannot stop the use of effective medical therapies in order to undertake environmental restructuring any more than we can ignore the sick of today to concentrate on the health of future populations. Whilst unreal they do, I think, make clear that the choices are essentially political choices which require to be based on the social values of citizens, rather than on the negotiations of the medical work-force. Professional expertise becomes relevant and essential, not only in the implementation of politically-made choices but in the delineation of the possible. I have referred passingly to a few of the many voices criticizing in recent years the unevaluated use of dubious or ineffective medical therapies. Medicine, however, may well be in a better position to evaluate the potentialities and the limits of medical intervention than either epidemiologists or social scientists can evaluate social action. McKeown could correctly conclude that social improvements had done more than medicine to improve health in the UK during the nineteenth and early twentieth centuries. But what he was evaluating had already spontaneously happened. It is a different thing making it happen. We know that our methods of health promotion and disease-prevention are crude in theory and weak in achievement. For years we have lacked the political will and the ability to discriminate positively in favour of depressed areas and classes and to legislate against disease-provoking agents and behaviour. We must also acknowledge that experiments in social action have either failed in action or have not produced the expected benefits. Political choice therefore depends upon scientific expertise as well as upon political will. Past under-emphasis on those very strategies to which the future points has weakened the immediate prospect of their fruitful mobilization.

I have so frequently met the complaint that information systems were inadequate for planning purposes that I almost elevated it to the level of a self-evident truth. It is not, however, a complaint frequently made by sociologists, who tend to use administrative statistics sparingly believing that, being derived from administrative practice, they have limited usefulness in answering sociological questions. In most fields the lack of good data means the past lack of people asking good questions. Parallel with Archie Cochrane in the field of clinical therapy, I believe that in the field of health and social services the deficiency is the absence of evaluative research (see chapter 6). Evaluation, in its many forms, and especially as a concomitant of innovatory programmes, is both a means of deciding what is practicable, efficient, and effective, but is also a spur to action. No informed choices can be made by governments, administrators, practitioners, or the public except against a constant background of evaluative work.

Evaluation has a place, as a routine continuous exercise, at all levels. Medical audit has a toe-hold. Is there such a thing as social services or social work audit? The evaluation of health services is still pursued erratically, typically resulting from the chance coincidence of an interested clinician or administrator, an available and interested research worker and the funds of the Chief Scientist Organization. My main concern is at the level of Health Boards and Health Departments where strategic decisions must be made and from which vantage point a strategic viewpoint across the service is possible. Yes, there are internal inquiries, memoranda and the reports of Working Parties but this largely internally-circulated material, drawing heavily on experience and on administrative statistics, is no substitute for scientific evaluation. Nor is it a good basis or good practice for the education of the public towards the making of informed choices between major options. Organizations cannot of course make available to the public what they do not possess. Another interpretation is that Boards and Departments prefer to operate as closed systems, perhaps reflecting the opinion that the issues are too complicated for public debate. There is now evidence to suggest that Health Council members get restricted access to information and that Board (Authority) members play a very limited role in policy-making (Kogan, 1968; Hunter, 1979).

The question of priorities, their determination and their

implementation, is thus inevitably linked to the question of evaluation, because evaluation is the process by which problems in the existing functioning of services are identified, options are revealed and weighed against each other and new policies are formulated and put into operation. Current thought and practice are deficient in several important respects.

(a) They rely unduly upon a mixture of administrative statistics and common-sense judgement.

(b) Undue attention is paid to outcome rather than process although it is becoming obvious that process determines outcome.

(c) Most evaluative activity is conducted internally by employees of Health Boards and Health Departments and especially in the case of Health Boards there is little external comparison with other areas and other services.

(d) Audiences affected by evaluative decisions (e.g. the general public, other parts of the health system, and other public services) do not have the knowledge and are not educated into the role of making informed choices about options which are frequently social, economic, and political in both their content and their implications. The total inability of senior clinical and research staff outside the Government (let alone the public) to get copies of a report prepared by the Central Policy Review Staff on alternative policies towards the legislative and fiscal control of alcoholism and smoking (presumably because Departments were divided and policies ineffectual) is one clear example of the over-secretive handling of policy issues.

The Royal Commission on the NHS approached these issues throughout their report and considered several possible solutions. They were primarily concerned with the unwieldiness of DHSS, accountability and financial control, and relations between central government and local health authorities. They did, however, make a number of references to the points I have just made.

We have some comments on the way NHS priorities are determined. First, we believe it is important that the lay public should be involved in the process. The discussion should not be left solely to health professionals and administrators, though we recognise that policies and priorities must be realistic and reflect what can be achieved, and must therefore take account of the views of professional and administrative staff in the NHS on their feasibility and likely consequences. . . .We recommend that more of the professional advice on which policies and priorities are based should be made public. This would strengthen the authority of the advice issued and lead to its readier acceptance in the field as well as promoting public discussion. (p. 53).

. . . but even after listening to careful explanations by representatives of the DHSS about the way in which the needs of particular priority groups are taken into account in the allocation of resources to health authorities, we remain mystified. We are bold enough to think that this is because there is some cloudiness in the Department's thinking about these matters, which are as important as anything in the Department's care. (p. 56).

The present national priorities . . . are not the result of objective analysis but of subjective judgment. Our view is that they are broadly correct at the present time, but they are certainly not the only possible choices. It is important to recognise that national priorities emerge from a variety of conflicting views and pressures expressed in Parliament, by the health professions and various patient or client pressure groups amongst others. So far as possible discussion which leads to the establishment of priorities should be conducted in public and illuminated by fact. (p. 69).

Discussing suggestions for 'taking the NHS out of politics':

Obviously there are aspects of the nation's health which would be better left out of *party* politics, but we believe it is both inevitable and right that the affairs of the NHS should be kept firmly at the centre of public debate. (p. 300).

Too often national policies have been advocated [by DHSS] without critically evaluated local experiment. (p. 304).

Discussing the maintenance of standards of care, the need to monitor services and to make priorities stick:

The necessary priorities will not be established at any level of the NHS unless there is strong continued public concern and pressure. . . . If health ministers and health authorities are unable to monitor services effectively within the structure then we suggest that stronger measures may be called for. One possibility would be to set up an independent special health authority for the purpose. (p. 309).

The Commission decided not to recommend the establishment of such a body at this time but the unease was clearly there. Apart from many minor and semi-exhortatory recommendations they did suggest setting up two bodies whose contribution might be relevant. The first was a Parliamentary Select Committee, 'properly served, with the power to examine health ministers, civil servants and expert witnesses'. The second, and unrelated proposal was for an independently-financed Institute of Health Services Research which would undertake specific research projects and would 'encourage the development of a corpus of knowledge and experience in the sphere of health services research, and could help to coordinate the research undertaken by universities and other agencies'. They quote with approval evidence submitted to the effect that 'To be of real value such research would have to be sponsored at a high level and undertaken by bodies of sufficient standing and independence to commend general support and acceptance'.

My own view is that some combination of these proposals is better than either taken separately. The Commission's acknowledgement that priorities should be established by discussion and that discussion 'should be conducted in public and illuminated by fact' is pertinent. A Select Committee has power and visibility but the views of health ministers, civil servants, and expert witnesses may produce a somewhat shuttered illumination. Research has little power and is more frequently ignored than adopted. The particular combination of a Parliamentary Select Committee and an Institute of Health Services Research is an unlikely hybrid but the principle of combining authority, independence, and visibility with monitoring and evaluation is valid. If we accept that structural reorganization has a relatively uncertain impact on behaviour; that a highly skilled workforce needs to be induced and motivated rather than driven; that pressures need to come from outside as well as inside the NHS; that the major issues concern moral and political judgements by an informed public, there are very few positive alternatives available. Such a body would need power, resources, and expertise to identify and monitor the development and implementation of policy. It would need to stretch across both health and social policy. It would need to make use of administrative material and statistics but also to conduct first-hand research at national and local levels, both on existing services and their impact, and on the evaluation of innovative change. Finally, it would need that access to inner circles which few private researchers attain, enough independence to withstand antagonism, and enough expertise, and sympathy with the system and its workforce, to earn respect. With a budget consisting of a tiny fraction of the cost of the NHS, it would not be expensive in relation to the intransigence of the problems, the cost of the services, or even of the amounts devoted to bio-medical, health services and social science research.

6

The evaluation of
health services

Experiment, in the sense of a chosen and specific intervention whose consequences are evaluated against other chosen and specific courses of action (or no-action) has been a standard approach in the natural sciences during the last two centuries. Since the Second World War, particular virtue has been attached in medical research to one form of experiment, the randomized controlled trial with or without its blinding or double-blinding accompaniments. The principles, practice, and virtues of the techniques have been fully described by Archie Cochrane (1972) in a previous monograph of this series. It is a powerful research tool in its ability to demonstrate in appropriate circumstances the effect of an intervention and to exclude the confounding effect of either irrelevant external influences or the subjective preferences of the experimenter and the subject. The randomized controlled trial and its variants grew out of biochemical and pharmacological research in laboratory and hospital work. Evaluation, however, is now being increasingly used to identify and measure the impact of intervention across a range of social, educational, and medical activities and services. The question frequently arises as to how far strictly controlled experiments are feasible in social rather than laboratory conditions, what alternative evaluative techniques are theoretically available, and how far medical sociologists should become involved in evaluative research. Sociologists do frequently reject evaluative research, for reasons which are probably ideological, or the result of training based heavily on theory and lightly on methodology. They are likely to suggest that experimental techniques are rarely available in sociological research, that the strict input/output model implies a dichotomous determinism not applicable in social situations or that evaluative activity is not the sociologist's business, possibly because it does not require or permit the use of sociological knowledge and skills. It is therefore worth unpacking the concept of evaluation to see in what ways it is relevant to policy or to service organization and whether it is compatible with sociological research methodology.

The classic evaluative model, most clearly exemplified in the randomized controlled trial, has several distinctive features. These are:

1. The primary objective of the intervention can be unequivocally specified.

2. It tests the effectiveness and/or efficiency of a given product or process in achieving the goal compared with alternative interventions or with no intervention.

3. It has a precise, foreseeable, and measurable control over the nature and quality of the input.

4. Influences extraneous to the measured input, the controlled intervention process, and the measured output can be excluded by research design.

5. The criterion of success is uncontroversial and can be measured on a single dimension.

These are stringent conditions which are rarely applicable outside the laboratory or the hospital ward. Even in the simpler situations to which the classical model should theoretically apply, these conditions frequently cannot be met, particularly where human subjects are concerned. Considerations of ethics, opinion, policy, or administration may prohibit either the experimental action itself, or its randomization; it may be impossible to ensure that all units of input are equal or measurable, or to exclude extraneous circumstances (e.g. other deliberate or accidental intervention, or disturbance of the physical or emotional state of the subject); it may not be possible to exclude awareness of the experimental process on the part of the experimentor or the subject and thus preclude subjective bias affecting input, output or their measurement; there may be no unequivocal measurable criterion of success as opposed to approximations, subjective estimates or the balancing of several advantages and disadvantages which cannot be reduced to a single scale. Side-effects or unintended consequences may not become immediately apparent. These, however, are technical limitations on how or when the method can be applied and as Cochrane (1972) shows they are, in theory, superable by refinements of technique, design or negotiation.

The sociologist, being a student of society, rather than a practitioner with a field of action and responsibility, will rarely get the opportunity to set up an experiment in social action. If he takes part in such an exercise his role is most likely to consist in formulating the theory which makes the experiment practicable or desirable and in assessing the social implications of whatever results emerge. Laboratory experiments involving the structure of groups, the processes of interaction, and the relationships between group members have been conducted by sociologists (more frequently by social psychologists) but the widespread belief persists that the design measures, the controlled conditions, and the unreality of the laboratory situation, render the processes and relationships under study significantly and incalculably different from occurrences in the external social world.

The more usual, and acceptable, situation confronting the sociologist is the observation of naturally-occurring social action. Similar questions are posed:

is this action achieving its stated goals?
or will this change in action produce a different or better outcome?
or does this organizational structure, set of procedures or cluster of activity produce a better outcome than some other specified set of conditions?

The differences methodologically are, firstly, that conditions are uncontrolled in that we are no longer dealing with a single input from which extraneous influences have been excluded—or even with a stated or shared set of goals and criteria of success; and secondly, that with the removal of limiting conditions there is a substantial increase in the range of situations susceptible to a looser form of evaluation.

In effect this means that instead of the researcher specifying his design and tailoring action to fit that design, he accepts action as it occurs and tailors his research design and methodology to produce the nearest approximation to experimental proof or scientific explanation. Four sets of circumstances occur in which limitations on action inhibit the use of rigorous experimental evaluation. These are:

1. Inability to determine goals
2. Inability to control input
3. Inability to measure or evaluate output
4. A combination of 1, 2 and 3.

There are, however, broader issues to be confronted before we can illustrate this more flexible form of evaluation. Practitioners of evaluation in the field of social action, social services, and health policy and health services (e.g. Caro, 1971; Suchman 1967) stress that evaluation is *not* something separate from service development or from research generally, but that it is a phase in service operation, reform and change. The process begins with (1) the identification and analysis of the operation of existing services and proceeds through (2) the specification of objectives, (3) the assessment of alternative strategies of change or reform to (4) the implementation of the reformed service to (5) evaluation of the effectiveness and efficiency of the new service and back again to the identification of new problems etc., etc. Evaluation should therefore ideally be an integral and continuing component of the organization and operation of a service. Occasions may arise in which the use of a randomized controlled trial will be indicated because service operation permits its use and because, for scientific ethical or policy reasons nothing short of a precise and definitive result is tolerable. This is clearly the case in evaluating the efficacy of drugs when laboratory development and testing have been completed, when safety problems have been solved, and when the only change of procedure indicated is the substitution of one drug for another. Such conditions however rarely arise in the routine organization of services and the danger exists that if evaluation is equated with this single methodology, which reduces the scientific task to a minimum but frequently creates major administrative problems for the service provider, then practitioners, policy-makers, and administrators will rarely find it possible to conduct evaluative work. A broader and less formal approach allows the service provider or policy-maker to evaluate the service continuously. This involves adopting a methodology which is practicable and acceptable during the uninterrupted provision of service, which can reasonably be expected to contribute to understanding relationships between input and output and which will give guidance on the next steps to be taken in the improvement of service. In many fields of action the innovative policy-maker finds it difficult to persuade service-providers to evaluate aspects of their service in the face of what has been called 'dynamic conservatism', i.e. fighting hard to remain in the same place.

The list of failures in evaluative work is formidable (Weiss, 1972; Elinson, 1972; Marris and Rein, 1967) and many such failures are attributable to the differing perspectives of service-providers and scientific research workers. Pre-occupied with his scientific methodology the research worker frequently wishes to impose upon the routine provision of service, conditions which are administratively troublesome, which cause ethical anxieties, and which reduce the freedom of clinical decision-making. The research worker, for reasons of experimental proof, may require the maintenance of the experiment or reform in its pure state long after it has become clear on commonsense grounds that modifications are called for. This both creates resistance to evaluation and tension between evaluator and service-provider. Regrettably the interests of the two do not always coincide.

The appropriateness of different types of evaluation depends upon the particular circumstances of the change or experiment involved. In many instances, particularly those involving social and political action, the evaluator has no choice about the nature, timing, and delivery of the input. Except in most unusual circumstances this is usually true of legislative change, e.g. legislation relating to licensing laws, seat belts, and abortion law reform. Quickly-mounted action may permit a rapid documentation of the before-stage (but research-funding procedures usually prohibit opportunistic research), previous research mounted for other purposes by other bodies may provide a background, but for the most part the impact of the legislation can be evaluated only by comparative study of variations arising out of its implementation in differing conditions of environment and organization, using the extraneous variables as research opportunities. Whilst in a scientifically-ordered society it might have been regarded as imperative that such measures be experimentally evaluated before their full implementation, in practice political and social values are crucial for the acceptance of such legislative reform and the naturally arising variations are the conditions under which the new service must operate. In this sense they are not extraneous variables but the inevitable accompaniments of change in a pluralistic society and cannot be controlled out.

Research workers may not be in a position to mount a post-hoc evaluation timeously; but this is a question of research organization, not of scientific methodology. There is no lack of sophisticated methodology. The topic has been exhaustively explored in the evaluative literature (Cook and Campbell, 1979; Webb, Campbell, Schwartz, and Sechrest 1966; Struening and Guttentag, 1975). Model designs have been evolved for use in field settings. The scientific aims of evaluators in field settings are no different from those of laboratory scientists or of the exponents of randomized controlled trials. They too are concerned with proof, evidence, validity, reliability, etc. The language of such literature however reveals the nature of their adaptation to imposed conditions. Here one meets such terms as approximations to knowledge, quasi-experimentation, interpretable comparisons, inductive evidence and causal inference, as enforced substitutes for cause-and-effect experimental proof. Webb et al (1966) quote Cardinal Newman's phrase 'From symbols and shadows to truth' to characterize the process of intelligently using available situations, data, and methodology to produce best approximations to the otherwise unknowable relationships between cause and effect or between input and output. Similarly in discussions of project design and of data, instead of RCTs and unequivocal measurement of a single outcome, one meets non-equivalent group design (with or without controls), interrupted time-series designs and triangulation (the simultaneous use of several sets of partial observations or perspectives focused upon a common problem). And the data-collection methods used are as variable as those used in general sociological research—historical evidence, index numbers, documents, records and files, interview and survey, and simple and participant observation. On both the data and the statistical methods used Webb et al (1966) approvingly quote the statistician Binder as follows:

We must use all available weapons of attack, face our problems realistically and not retreat to the land of fashionable sterility, learn to sweat over our data with an admixture of judgment and intuitive rumination, and accept the usefulness of particular data even when the level of analysis available for them is markedly below that available for other data in the empirical area. (Binder, 1964).

How far are the conditions which necessitate such approximations and multiple methodologies applicable to research on health policy and health services? The answer depends on the view taken about three other questions:

1. To what extent are these areas open or closed systems—in the sense that conditions relating to the experiment, reform, or change are able to be controlled, and extraneous influences removed?

2. What is being evaluated? An existing service or a reformed service? A system of delivery or stages and components of a system? A precisely measurable input, or inputs of a multiple and interdependent nature, or involving a proportion of judgements and degrees of potential compliance or deviation?

3. What is the nature of the presumed outcome? For example, are the alternative outcomes known in advance and with what degree of precision? Is the likely outcome a single measurable quantity, e.g. a mortality rate? Or are we dealing with multiple outcomes, requiring judgement, balancing, and ranking, or outcomes not directly measurable? Is the outcome likely to vary between settings and is there agreement about the criteria of success?

These questions about open and closed systems, what is being evaluated and what are the criteria of success are themselves inter-related but they can be discussed separately for heuristic purposes. On the first question my position is that health policy and health services research deals overwhelmingly with open systems similar in kind to those involving political and social action. This generalization needs to be qualified by at least one further generalization namely that in the spectrum from evaluation of a system change (e.g. the 1974 reorganization of the NHS) to evaluation of a single change of treatment, the nearer we approach the 'closed' situation in which trials become possible. Examples drawn from this spectrum are given below.

ADENO-TONSILLECTOMY

In this discussion of RCTs, Cochrane gives illustrations of successful trials but also gives wistful brief accounts of ones that 'got away'. Among the latter he includes tonsillectomy. The problem is an old one. Few proponents of adeno-tonsillectomy today would claim for the operation the somewhat magical effects thought possible at the turn of the century when it was fast becoming considered 'a panacea for all the ills of a child whose tonsils project beyond the anterior pillar of his fauces', (Layton, 1914). A more modest contemporary claim might be that adeno-tonsillectomy prevents or reduces sore throats, tonsillitis, and cervical adenitis, and that it reduces the frequency of otitis media and associated deafness.

Three RCTs have been conducted in the UK with contradictory results about whether they did or did not reduce upper respiratory infection or otitis media. Cochrane correctly points to the technical limitations of each trial and particularly to two features, (1) that comparison was between 'operation' and 'inadequate medical treatment' rather than between the best surgical and best medical treatments, and (2) that post-operation success was not based on 'direct evidence' but upon parents' accounts of their child's health and that such accounts might well have been biased because parents had favoured this treatment. He concludes:

The present situation is therefore very unsatisfactory. It will probably be some time before a perfect controlled trial, without bias, and with adequate medical treatment, is mounted. At the present there seems every reason to limit tonsillectomy to cases of obstruction. No case should be placed on a surgical waiting-list but always referred for medical treatment, and only when this fails after a prolonged trial should the case be sent to the surgeon. This should reduce the number of tonsillectomies to about one-fifth of the present numbers.

In other words, in the absence of a perfect RCT, the answer is not evaluative research of other kinds but decisions based on personal judgement.

Adeno-tonsillectomy, however, poses a number of additional questions. Concern arises, not because of the adverse effects of the operation (although some deaths do occur and some adverse post-operative effects are claimed), but because it may be ineffective and because in these circumstances much unnecessary expense and pain will have been caused. Epidemiological research as far back as the 1930s showed enormous variations in the operation rate between local authority districts (Glover, 1938). Whilst the total operation rate has undoubtedly decreased, considerable inter-area variability remains, and few would suggest that this geographical variation reflects variability in symptomatology. Glover's (1948) opinion that 'these great variations in local incidence . . . appear to depend entirely upon medical opinion in the individual area' would receive widespread informed support.

One question to be addressed in a full evaluation of the adeno-tonsillectomy issue would be that implied by Cochrane, namely, 'Is tonsillectomy more effective than the best available medical treatment in the prevention or mitigation of upper respiratory disease and each of its related manifestations?' Other questions, however, also require answers. Why do operation rates vary between districts and between surgeons or surgical services? What is the variation in referral rates from general practitioners to surgical services? What criteria are used by practitioners and surgeons in assessing the need for intervention? or the desirability of adeno-tonsillectomy as opposed to medical treatment, no treatment or postponement of decision about treatment? Do clinicians use the same criteria? Do they vary in the application of these criteria? Do clinicians follow up and evaluate their own treatment and what criteria of success do they apply?

In a joint epidemiological-sociological study of adeno-tonsillectomy carried out in Scotland, Bloor and Venters (1979) plot the pathways towards adenotonsillectomy followed by the child (Fig. 6.1). They comment:

To reach adeno-tonsillectomy children must be perceived as sick by their parents, be seen by a family doctor who believes in the beneficial nature of the operation, attain that level of illness which the family doctor considers an indication for referral, have willing parents, be referred to an ENT specialist, be considered by the specialist to merit operation, and suffer sufficiently between the time of decision to operate and that when the bed is available for the child's admission, for all concerned to agree to the operation.

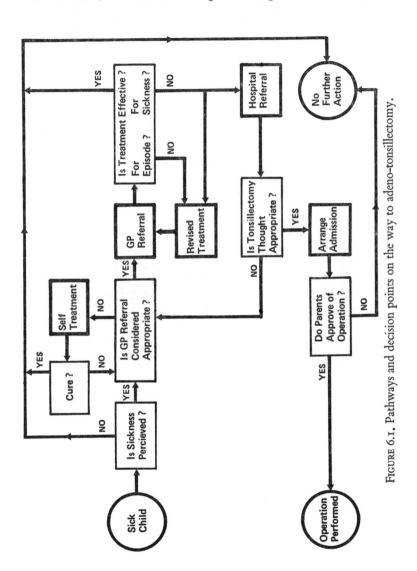

FIGURE 6.I. Pathways and decision points on the way to adeno-tonsillectomy.

At each divergent point in the pathway a decision must be made and criteria of some kind must be employed in reaching that decision. A full evaluation of 'the adeno-tonsillectomy service' would require that each decision point be studied. Admittedly if a perfect trial were conducted, directed at the clinical question of the efficacy of adeno-tonsillectomy, many of the prior questions relating to process might become scientifically redundant. In an imperfect world, however, the possibility of mounting a perfect trial and producing unequivocal answers capable of clear application, seems remote. Moreover, given the general agreement, among many observers over many years, that a substantial proportion of operations are unnecessary and the high (but falling) frequency of both the operation and of large inter-district specialist variations, one may justifiably ask whether a scientific answer to the clinical question of efficacy would be a sufficient ground for a radical change of practice.

Bloor and Venters, in what they agree is only a limited study of practice in two Scottish Regions, demonstrated:

1. That annual rates of referral for possible adeno-tonsillectomy ranged between general practices from 4·4 to 31·3 per 1000 children per practice. Although city group practices referred significantly more than other type practices, there were no significant differences between group and non-group practices nor between city and rural practices; they concluded that GP assessment practices rather than type and location of practice were the main sources of variation in referral rates.

2. That the proportion of cases assessed that were eventually listed for surgery varied between specialists from 46 per cent to 85 per cent.

3. That the differences between regions resulted from the proportion of specialists who were low or high acceptors and from the case-load allocation between high and low acceptors in each region.

4. That inter-specialist variation resulted from the fact that each specialist followed his own established routine assessment practice in making disposal decisions.

Bloor observed and analysed these assessment practices and identified two classes of variation, one proceeding from the 'search procedure' used in eliciting the history of symptoms, severity, and frequency, and the other from the 'decision-rules' applied to the data thus obtained. For example, in cases of possible T and A he noted variation in the particular clinical signs taken into account; variation in the stress placed on examination evidence relative to the clinical history; variation in the search procedures used in history-taking and in the decision rules pertaining to the history; variation in the propensity to defer for later review, and variation in the routines for children at different ages. On the basis of these findings Bloor and Venters (1980) point out that there is no reason why a specialist should modify his practice as a result of an RCT—except in the unlikely situation that the trial used working definitions of the appropriate indications similar to those he used himself. Since working definitions vary so widely each clinical trial would need to be preceded by a careful study of everyday practice and modified to fit each set of circumstances.

The investigators were not performing 'an evaluation of adeno-tonsillectomy'. They were however doing evaluative research of the kind which is frequently necessary in evaluating a health service as opposed to a drug or a treatment. In applying sociological observation and analysis to a process involving successive decisions on the part of parents, general practitioners, and specialists and in comparing the different contexts of decision-making they were also identifying the points at which control would have to be exercised in any subsequent RCT. A fuller evaluation, with more policy-oriented objectives, would need to study the part played by adeno-tonsillectomy work in the total load of ENT surgeons and their reasons for using their time-resources on this as opposed to other clinical tasks.

ANTENATAL CARE

Another health service area where a call has been made for an RCT is that of antenatal care. In recent years some individuals and organizations, disappointed in the slow decline of the UK perinatal death rate, have claimed that deaths would be avoided and the perinatal death rate lowered by the provision of more and better antenatal care. If the suggestion is that death rates would be appreciably affected and that lack of adequate antenatal care is responsible for a relative deterioration in perinatal death in the UK compared with some other European countries, the suggestion should be treated with some scepticism. It is, of course, correct that perinatal death rates are lower in aggregate for women who report early for antenatal care and who attend regularly for care. This conclusion however is largely based upon crude correlations and it does not follow that early and regular attendance itself produces better results, that late attendance in itself causes death or that more antenatal care would prevent deaths. It has been known for many years (Illsley, 1956b) that women who attend late and irregularly are partially self-selected and that in general they carry higher risks because of poorer growth and physique, because their diet and housing conditions are poorer, and because they are drawn disproportionately from sub-groups, e.g. unmarried mothers, subject to special risks. The relationship of living standards and environmental experience to efficient reproductive performance is also well-established and it would be surprising if, as gross national product per capita in the UK declined relative to that of our European neighbours, we were able to maintain the superiority in reproductive mortality and morbidity which we enjoyed at earlier periods. Explanation of the causes of comparative shifts in ranking between European countries would require a much more rigorous and comprehensive analysis than has yet been attempted and would have to take into account age, parity, maternal height, weight, diet, smoking habits, and physical activity. Data on antenatal care would need to specify not only date and frequency of attendance but the details of care and treatment received and the responses to treatment. Care in labour and the puerperium would need equally detailed documentation and the results would need to look at complications and morbidity as well as death classified by clinical cause.

Apart from the self-selection and differential characteristics of mothers attending early or late there are other grounds for doubting the marginal effect of antenatal care upon outcome. Some complications carrying above average mortality risks (e.g. pre-eclampsia, malpresentation) cannot be predicted with any degree of certainty until the third trimester or even into labour itself. Intra-uterine growth retardation has a higher detection rate (again predominantly in the third trimester) but the potentialities of treatment are extremely limited even when correctly predicted. Premature delivery is equally difficult to detect in advance and to prevent. Careful and initial screening certainly pays dividends. In general, however, there are grounds for caution against over-optimistic expectations of any substantial lowering of death rates through either early or more antenatal care.

An excellent case exists, however, for a detailed evaluation of the various and specified components of antenatal care. Such an evaluation might suggest that more, or more skilled and intensive, attention be paid to particular risk-factors, it might suggest improved administrative and monitoring procedures—it might, however, also suggest that some components of antenatal care were unproductive and wasteful. An inexpensive evaluative study of this type was carried out by Dr Marion Hall (1980), consultant obstetrician, and Dr Chng, Research Fellow, using the routine records and case sheets of the Aberdeen Maternity Service. Drs Hall and Chng started with the justified assumption that evaluation of the existing service logically preceded change and the evaluation of change. The framework and general objectives of their study were described as follows: 'A proper appraisal of antenatal care must take account of the epidemiology of obstetric complications, their predictability, detectability and preventability in theory and in practice, and the cost to the patient and the health service of such a programme'.

They argued that a review of the problems attributable to the patients, those attributable to the clinicians, as well as those due to the unpredictable nature of some obstetric complications, would identify any limitations of the existing system of antenatal care; and, if necessary, suggest modifications to achieve a more efficient system, in which personnel and investigative resources are more properly deployed. The investigators then carried out the following documentation and analyses:

1. gestation at first antenatal visit for the total population and

for sub-groups defined by social class, parity and marital status; status of doctor (consultant, senior registrar etc.) seen at first visit and the degree to which the doctor recognized significant features of past medical and obstetric history.

2. differential allocation of high and low-risk patients for delivery at the major hospital or at maternity homes, and the perinatal death rates of high and low-risk patients,

3. transfers of booking to major hospital either antenatally or in labour, and the degree to which the factors leading to transfer could have been predicted at booking.

4. number and phasing of antenatal visits throughout pregnancy and number of different doctors seen,

5. failure to attend for care on arranged dates analysed by factors of possible relevance,

6. the detection rate at each stage of pregnancy of major asymptomatic complications (pre-eclampsia, intra-uterine growth retardation, breech) and the calculation of productivity of visits at each gestation stage in respect of detection, under-detection, and over-detection of these complications,

7. emergency admissions and operations and degree to which they were predictable on basis of available information,

8. productivity in terms of true and false positives of each routine or selective investigation or test (including height, weight gain, and blood pressure).

Such analyses enabled the investigators to reach conclusions about actual clinical productivity of each antenatal visit and each investigation in terms of true detection of major complications, the degree to which major complications and mortality risk could have been detected in the antenatal stage, the degree to which emergency transfers could have been avoided and the number of cases in which attempted prediction produced false-positive judgements. For example, the majority of antenatal admissions to hospital (other than for delivery) were for conditions which had arisen in spite of antenatal care and were not prevented or detected by it. For every genuine case of pre-eclampsia diagnosed at least one case was found of hypertension which settled and was of no clinical significance. Furthermore, pre-eclampsia presented for the first time in labour or in the puerperium (i.e. after the antenatal period) in as many as 3 out of 10 cases. Intrauterine growth retardation which must have been present during the antenatal period was detected by the clinician in less than half the cases: and for every woman correctly predicted as having a growth retarded baby, another 2·5 were so predicted without having the condition. Such over-diagnosis may lead to over-investigation and unnecessary admission, induction or operative delivery. Half of the cases of perinatal death had no risk-factor identifiable at booking.

A parallel sociological study by Dr S. Macintyre (1979) showed that most women knew very little about the purposes of antenatal care and of the procedures to which they were subjected. They felt the need for more information and discussion, not only about professionally conducted antenatal care, but also about wider aspects of pregnancy, childbirth, and parenthood and their own role and participation in the process. Study of their travelling time and of the arrangements necessary to attend the clinic showed that many women incurred high social and/or economic costs.

The investigators concluded by questioning the need for normal asymptomatic women to attend so often for routine examination. They suggested a rearranged schedule of visits, different for primigravidae and timed to the gestation periods at which specified complications became detectable and at which intervention is possible or appropriate. Apart from increasing the productivity of visits the new schedule allows greater opportunity for the discussion, reassurance, and education shown by the sociological study to be desirable. After lengthy discussion, the area clinical obstetricians, midwives and general practitioners accepted the recommendations and decided to implement the new arrangements *tout court*. They explicitly ruled out a randomized controlled trial on both ethical and administrative grounds and because no single clear-cut intervention or outcome could be specified. Dr Hall has now prepared a second evaluative exercise, comparable to the previous one and involving both clinical and sociological investigations, to monitor the functioning of the new system.

I cite this example because it illustrates many features of evaluative work in the field of health services.

1. It began with the analysis of existing problems, conceived within an epidemiological framework, and proceeded through evaluation of the existing services, reconsideration of objectives, recommendations for change, and implementation and back to evaluation. It was not therefore a one-off exercise but an integral part of the conduct and monitoring of a service.

2. It recognized that antenatal care is composed of many elements each of which needed examination both separately and as part of a comprehensive service. The question was not whether more or better antenatal care was necessary but whether some elements were more or less productive, whether effort was being directed efficiently to the items of service and the points of gestation where risk could be identified and effective intervention made.

3. The core topic of evaluation was not the efficiency and effectiveness of a single investigation, method of treatment or operation, but of the administrative procedures within which each of these single items was embedded. Rather than ruling out issues normally defined as extraneous to a clinical/scientific question, it incorporated them as an integral component. In so doing the study identified, but did not address itself to, problems concerning the effectiveness of specific clinical activities, e.g. the adequacy of risk criteria used in the allocation of patients to the major hospital as opposed to maternity homes, or the low rate of detection of intra-uterine growth retardation. They are proper subjects for study and the investigation revealed the need for such study, but they are not necessary components of an evaluation addressed to the administrative arrangements for the delivery of a service as opposed to its internal components. Evaluation of such single items would require different study designs, perhaps approximating more to the conventional methods of scientific trials.

4. It recognized that the objectives of different participants in the service, patients, obstetricians, midwives, and general practitioners, did not necessarily coincide and that patients were not a homogeneous group with identical needs. It therefore made use of sociological material about the differential perceptions of the participants and these will be further monitored in evaluation of the restructured service. In optimal conditions an RCT

produces a clear-cut answer based on the logic of biochemical processes and in which the case for the implementation of findings is unarguable. In the delivery of a service clear-cut answers and unarguable logic are rarely attainable because participants have different roles and different objectives, because a change in one part of a system produces a range of repercussions in other parts, and finally and perhaps most important, because we are dealing with the choice between alternative strategies each of which may have its advantages and disadvantages. In the present instance there is a tension between the most convenient arrangements for conducting a busy routine service, the wish to ensure safety by insisting on frequent attendance and comprehensive investigations, the need to motivate patients to attend early and regularly and the desire of patients for more personal continuity, more information and discussion, and a minimization of the social and economic costs of attendance.

One reason for the willingness of professionals to implement the recommendations of this evaluative exercise was that it was based upon and proceeded outwards from the existing service and its problems, that it took account of differential perceptions and that it enabled a reformed system to continue without interruption of service and without the major inconvenience frequently attendant upon randomization and control. Overall, the study demonstrates that successive partial evaluations and reforms are superior to perfect trials which demand such stringent conditions that they cannot be carried out.

THE IMPLEMENTATION OF HEALTH POLICY

Policy research has experienced a long debate about how decisions *are* or *should be* made (the two questions, as Smith and May (1980) point out, are qualitatively different). If we wish to evaluate policy some understanding is required of two opposing models of decision-making. The rationalist model postulates the following four steps in the policy decision-making process:

1. a search to discover goals
2. the formulation of objectives after search

3. the selection of alternatives (strategies) to accomplish objectives

4. the evaluation of outcomes

Furthermore it assumes that in both the search for objectives and in the selection of alternatives a review will be made of the whole range of possible objectives and alternatives. Smith and May summarize five criticisms of the model derived from theoretical and empirical work on organizations: First, 'most decision-makers in policy contexts do not work in an environment free of constraints. They are simply not free to consider all possible options and are compelled to short-list, if not actually recommend, options that they would not even pretend to justify as the most appropriate in terms of a simple means–end schema'. Second, the model is utopian in that, in the real world, 'ends are not that clear, decisions are not that neat, and evaluation is not that systematic. Indeed it has been argued that ambiguity is actually a rather central feature of most policy and should be acknowledged and studied as such'. Third, the approach is value-biased in that what is rational depends upon objectives and it is likely that the objectives of management and professionals will be the criteria embodied in the policy. Fourth, the distinction between ends and means, values and decisions, and facts and values are too rigidly drawn. In practice means and ends are often chosen simultaneously within the administrative process. Finally, the approach is impractical in that a review of all relevant objectives and alternative strategies together with all relevant data is impossible to carry out.

The alternative incrementalist approach meets some of these criticisms in accepting that in the real world the policy maker starts with existing policies and constraints and builds outward making incrementalist changes at the margin. The approach is criticized as conservative in that it reinforces existing structures and ideologies rather than seeking radical alternatives and optimal solutions.

These two approaches and the criticisms of them have several implications for the evaluation of health policy and of its implementation. If we accept (and much empirical work suggests that there are good grounds for so doing (Smith and May, 1980;

The evaluation of health services

Wiseman, 1978, 1979; Lindblom, 1959; Hall et al, 1975; and Hill, 1978), that ambiguity is a frequent feature of policy, that full-scale reviews rarely occur, that policy change occurs incrementally at the margin, that objectives vary across the system, then the formal approaches to evaluation are inoperable. It is not merely that trials cannot be conducted, let alone randomized or controlled, it is often impossible:

to locate the policy-maker,

to identify the precise nature of the problems impelling change or an analysis of these problems,

to identify the alternative objectives and strategies reviewed or the constraints affecting choice,

to determine objectives adopted and the relationship between them in the hierarchy of objectives,

to determine the criteria of a successful policy and to decide whose objectives and criteria should have weight.

In these circumstances items which would normally define the agreed framework and parameters of the research design themselves become problematic and the subjects of research. The evaluator may have to interview retrospectively, examine files and documents, and carry out interviews or questionnaire surveys in order to specify the origins of the policy, the objectives and action strategies, and the success criteria perceived by a range of persons—each of whom may have a different definition of the situation. In tracing policy decisions through the system in order to study effort and impact the evaluator may have to repeat the process at many levels to understand how the policy was interpreted and modified, what constraints there were upon action, and what translations had occurred before it resulted in a reformulated service. Depending upon the nature of the policy and what is being evaluated, the measurement of impact (e.g. the effect on the number of vasectomies of giving surgeons a fee for the operation) may be the simplest part of the evaluation. If, however, we are concerned to understand the variability and degrees of implementation, the barriers to implementation, the unintended consequences in terms of diversion of resources from other activities, etc. then the evaluation is extremely complex.

The evaluation of health services

One recent study of such a complex set of issues provides an example of this more 'illuminative' type of evaluation. Starting from the proposition that central government policy had been notably unsuccessful in removing the imbalances between regions and health authorities, and between care groups and sectors of health care within health authorities, David Hunter (1980) questioned the widespread belief that the 1974 reorganization would result in more rational decision making. He noted the considerable influence still possessed by local health authorities over the service they provide and drew a distinction between the controls central government has over health authorities and their actual operation. It was clear that while middle-range decision-making at health board level might have an impact on broader, more strategic policy-making, it was often a substitute for such policy-making, precisely because of the difficulties experienced by decision-makers in adopting and implementing a more 'synoptic' 'rationalist' approach.

There are many possible ways of studying the effectiveness and efficiency of the policy process. One approach to some of the questions is to compare stated policies and priorities with their outcome. Mooney et al (1980) in a discussion of programme budgeting point out that 'it is all too easy for a health board or authority to become heavily engaged in *ad hoc* decisions on minor changes in resource allocation, in patching up deficiencies in individual services and in considering only the 3 per cent or so (and less in future) of development monies each year'. They calculate annual changes in expenditure on each major grouping of services over six years and are able to demonstrate degrees of conformity to or departure from certain priorities. The technique is clearly useful for planning purposes and particularly for prompting 'questions about those trends which give rise to some element of surprise or imbalance'.

Whilst such an approach has monitoring value, it does not claim to have explanatory power. Hunter focuses on the *process* by which financial resources were allocated to different ends and his case study sought 'answers to questions like the following: How are scarce resources allocated? Who is involved in these decisions? How are choices made between competing demands?

Is there a hierarchy of power or influence? What information is used in the discussions surrounding the decision-making process?' He attempted to answer these questions by studying, in two health board areas over two financial years, the process by which they allocated 'Development Funds'—the 'new' money which the boards then received from the Scottish Office to develop new services, improve existing ones, or to change direction as a result of guidance about new central priorities. His data were varied and differed considerably from the conventional data of scientific trials. They consisted of:

1. Notes of his personal attendance at and observation of meetings of strategic committees—the area executive group, district executive groups, professional advisory committees, and the policy and resources committees of the Board.

2. Data from semi-structured interviews with Board members, staff, professional advisors, and key civil servants, supplemented by casual chat around corridors and canteens.

3. All board and committee documents dealing with Development Funds and other relevant organizational and financial documents.

4. Data about comparable issues obtained by questionnaire from the other 13 Scottish Boards.

His analysis of these data reveals a fundamentally incrementalist approach. The chief officers of the Board (not the Board) set off a process whereby at sector level, the lowest administrative level consulted, heads of medical and other departments specified their new staff and other requirements for transmission to district level where lists were made up with some priority ranking before further transmission to the area level where the chief officer group allocated sums between districts and sent the lists back with suggestions for priorities. Then the process was repeated whereby chief officers revised and co-ordinated the district lists, sent them out to professional advisory committees for comment, and then revised them again for their submission to the Policy and Resources Committee of the Board. They finally arrived at the Board as agreed recommendations which the Board were asked to note.

Hunter's descriptive account shows how, through the process adopted, the agenda is set by the demands of existing services and how decision-making consists of Board officers managing the conflict between particular interests, using a 'fair shares' approach, giving a little more here and there. Whilst conscious of central policies, their most difficult task was to resolve the conflict of competing interests created by their own request for recommendations. In resolving the conflict they used value criteria of equity and balance rather than principles derived from the rationalist model, i.e. a review of existing services, determination of objectives, consideration of all alternative strategies, etc. At the end of the process there was some marginal scope for implementing the priority guidelines but this appeared as the residual outcome rather than the prime objective.

Hunter (1980a) stresses several important features of his research strategy. Firstly he neither just observed nor did he set up tight hypotheses for testing. He conducted a thorough review of relevant theories and concepts and applied them in a loose eclectic approach drawing upon them wherever they assisted in illuminating a particular fragment of the story of development fund allocations. This gave him the advantage of a multi-paradigmatic approach based on the premise that all tools of explanation explain something, but that none explain everything in such a complex policy process.

Secondly he points out that, by studying the process as it occurred he was able to challenge the common assumption that policy operates in a top-downwards hierarchical fashion. In highly professionalized activity like health services where local service providers have considerable discretionary powers, policy is frequently *made* at the periphery by those ostensibly responsible for implementing it. Reform based on the idea that policy proceeds downwards through the hierarchy is likely to focus on ways of reducing the slippage between the expectations of policy-makers on high and the reality on the ground, and to prompt changes in structure and organization, in communication channels, and in monitoring and control procedures. If policy is made at the periphery, such reforms are likely to fail unless they simultaneously take account of the interests, perceptions, and powers of those responsible for implementing central policy.

In the traditional and formal sense Hunter was not conducting an evaluation. In practice, his case-studies do evaluate the process by which policy is implemented, both against the objectives of policy and against implicit assumptions about the rationalist nature of the implementation process. The data are not cut and dried in the tradition of the natural sciences, instead they trace and reflect what is and must be a fragmented, complex process. The data have to be put together and the process reconstructed with various forms of logical analysis but also with judgements about the relative weight and influence of actors and items. The study, therefore, goes well beyond the normal purpose of a trial which is to confirm or deny a hypothesized relationship between input and output derived from pre-existing theory. The task of relating an input (development funds) to output (a resource allocation) produces simultaneously an explanatory model of how the system works. This kind of research has correctly been called 'illuminative evaluation'. Most sociologists would not regard it as a distinct genre of research, but merely as a sociological study of process, characterized by its policy-orientation and its explanatory aims, but not by its methodology. I consider that, as scientific attention turns from laboratory conditions and drug or operative intervention to the study of health services and policy change, where formal trials are most often impracticable or unrevealing, sociological research of this kind will become increasingly for evaluating purposes necessary.

7

The methodology of sociology

Discussions between sociologists and natural or medical scientists rarely proceed for long without questions being raised about the reliability and validity of sociological data and analytical methods. The most common criticism relates to the sociologist's use of 'soft' methods. It is typically argued that sociological data are subject to observer selectivity, bias or error, that they cannot be reliably replicated, that they are often based on small numbers, and that measurement is imprecise. As a result, the sociologist is at liberty to select interpretations convenient to his argument or ideology and the reader is unable to differentiate fact from opinion, or to re-check the analysis to test competing hypotheses. Moreover, by necessarily relying on inference and deduction, sociological study cannot advance cause-and-effect relationships or build up a body of defensible general laws. It would be dishonest to deny that there is some truth in these methodological criticisms. I have myself used almost all of them many times and they are used as frequently by sociologists as by their critics.

It is important to distinguish between what some sociologists do and what constitutes sociology in the minds and practice of its acknowledged masters. The subject matter of sociology is the social, economic, and political world in which we live and is attractive to ideologues, honest and dishonest, scientific and non-scientific, precisely because of this closeness to real-world issues. The intrusion of personal opinion and beliefs, of judgements resting upon pre-conceived ideas and values, is not uncommon in any science dealing with human affairs. It is also common in applied sciences, particularly where missing elements of knowledge have to be supplemented by inference and approximation to make action possible. Medicine could hardly be practised if such judgements were foresworn.

My acceptance, and that of other sociologists, of the kind of criticisms advanced above rests on grounds which are applicable over a wide range of human enquiry. It springs from doubts about the knowableness of the social world. The fundamental issue is clearly older than sociology. Indeed, it has formed part of philosophical disputation for as long as philosophy has existed and has reduced some modern schools of philosophy into what are often seen as sterile arguments about language. In previous chapters I have frequently used the words 'social structure' to refer to a collection of institutions, activities and relationships, and culturally accepted norms and beliefs. We (and not only sociologists) use this term as a convenient summary of endless patterned activities which we know, in commonsense terms, differ from place to place and time to time. There is, of course, no structure, the term being symbolic, and drawn from our experience of the physical world. As an intellectual creation it appears differently to individuals viewing the world from different positions, experience, and perspectives. This creates several problems for the sociologist who must get behind the similarity of terminology to the different definitions employed by each informant, not only in the sense of its empirical referents but also the implicit theorizing, and its relationship to the beliefs, activity, expectations, and daily life of the individual. Diversity of definition and meaning are perhaps most to be expected in the use of such a general term as 'social structure', but we have also seen that 'illness' contains a similar diversity, that 'family', 'illegitimacy', and 'abortion' have culturally different and historically changing meanings. Action does not spring from social laws—on the contrary such laws only have validity if they capture and encapsulate the actions themselves, the meanings attached to them by 'actors', and the rules which they implicitly or explicitly follow.

From this perspective, social meanings (which direct human behaviour) do not inhere in activities, institutions or social objects themselves. Rather meanings are conferred upon social events by inter-acting individuals, who must first interpret what is going on from the social context in which these events occur. (Schwartz and Jacobs, 1979).

Thus, regularities or patterns of behaviour obtained by observing how individuals and groups typically respond to particular social situations become merely the entry point to an understanding of subjective perceptions. My emphasis in earlier chapters on the need for open-minded and detailed observation and study of life-styles, and orientations to illness follows on the requirement that sociological knowledge should be built up from first-hand evidence of this kind.

In interpreting social action sociologists have an intrinsic advantage over the natural scientist studying animal behaviour or molecular activity. Because their subjects are also human beings, they have their own personal insight into meanings, motivations, and the rules that govern social action. The advantage is double-edged. Human beings other than sociologists theorize about social action, and as informants they typically interweave their accounts of events, attitudes, and relationships with explanations of why and how. Even more difficult, scientifically, is the danger that, in carrying this inside knowledge into the field and their offices, sociologists will interpret events from their own perspective and impose patterns and interpretations irrelevant to the world of their subjects.

The history of sociology is littered with discussion and conflict, not only over the existence and importance of a real objective social world or one of subjective meanings, but also about the validity of methodological approaches to finding out about the world. The varieties of sociological methods reflect the theoretically-based attempts of practitioners to 're-construct reality' in the face of these uncertainties. It is particularly irritating to a discipline so methodologically conscious that external critics feel able to produce critical judgements which, based on scientific developments in quite different contexts, are themselves methodologically naive. In my experience medical and natural scientists are usually most comfortable with the so-called 'hard' data of structured social surveys and administrative statistics. They produce 'social facts' generated and collected under known circumstances, visible and capable of being re-worked by other scientists and based on large enough numbers to rule out chance errors and to be subdivided by other administrative statistics and other social facts such as age, sex, residence, and occupation. I do not wish to 'knock' such data. I collect, use and benefit from them. The question of their hardness is another matter, as also are their meaning and interpretation.

The validity and reliability of data from structured social surveys are thought to rest upon the fact that, in identical survey conditions, they are responses to precisely worded questions administered according to precise rules. Like a carefully controlled laboratory experiment the input, in the form of questions, is visible and can be seen to be standardized, inter-interviewer error can be measured, the number of interviews necessary to achieve significant results can be calculated in advance, and another interviewer can attempt to replicate the responses on another set of respondents. Finally, results can be reduced to numbers and subjected to cross tabulation and statistical tests. The problem lies not in the data-processing but in the nature of the data. The collection of survey data is based on the assumption that the same question asked of persons who differ in many ways, will produce answers which, for each person, are equally revealing of their beliefs, attitudes, and behaviour. How far the question is interpreted and answered similarly, how far a standard question taps the experience, emotion, meaning, and salience of the topic and just what it reveals and what it fails to elicit is unknowable, not only to the interviewer, but also to the analyst and the reader. Social survey experts do have sophisticated techniques of piloting, question-framing and topic coverage designed to minimize the pitfalls. However, the more that questioning and follow-up are tailored to the particular individual by semi-structuring and variable ordering of questions, the more the exercise loses its standardized quality, the more difficult it becomes for the paid interviewer to take advantage of the clues offered—and the longer the interview becomes. Instead of the sociologist framing standardized questions in advance, reflective of his interests, he begins to approach the more open-ended situation in which talk around the topic reflects the respondent's interests, leaving the sociologist with a collection of interviews containing individualistic responses and with the methodological problem of abstracting and evaluating similarities, differences and patterns without imposing them on the analysis.

The methodology of sociology

Administrative statistics present equally difficult problems of validity. They are collected for purposes other than research and must above all else fulfil their own purpose. Use of data on simple yes–or–no events, a birth, a death, an admission, a discharge, presents few pitfalls except in the interpretation of the patterns they reveal, but equally they have limited value. Casenotes are more complex. They are compiled from action–oriented questioning in which facts not salient to the specific purpose are ignored. Their very recording is intended as reminders for future occasions, for the information of colleagues, or for demonstrating that correct procedures have been followed. Coded diagnostic categories are equally complex and they can be both meaningless and misleading for research purposes. Blaxter (1978) has shown that they depend upon a diagnosis having been made, upon the fullness of the doctor's recording, the choice of primary diagnosis, the adequacy of available ICD codings, and on the coder's translation of the diagnosis into an ICD category. Similarly, Douglas' (1967) re-examination of the processes by which a verdict of suicide is reached and recorded has converted Durkheim's (1897) classical model of a sociological/epidemiological analysis into a teacher's manual of methodological error.

Sociologists have responded to problems of epistemology and data validity by developing a range of approaches, from the expert manipulation of demographic facts and social survey methods through symbolic interactionism (taking the role of the other) to phenomenology and the attempt to approach the phenomena of the social world without importing the analyst's own preoccupations, assumptions, and values. For data collection, apart from simple social facts and statistics, there are variants of the social survey, degrees of in-depth interviewing of individuals or groups by sociologists themselves, historical sources and records, diaries, content analysis of the media and written material, simple observation and/or audio or visual recording of situations, relationships and activities, observation as a participant, and yet other techniques evolved for particular tasks. Experimental design is unusual because opportunities rarely occur, but the usual techniques are adapted to take advantage of natural experiments and innovatory action. Whatever the results, sociology can hardly be characterized as lacking methodological awareness and flexibility.

Sociological research is labour-intensive because, on the whole, one project means a minimum of one full-time professional for periods of up to three or more years and only limited tasks can be delegated to interviewers, clerical, and computing assistants. Without more funds or a fundamental re-organization of the research enterprise away from individualistic University research towards professional teams and Units, some desirable procedures tend to go by default. Partial replication can occur because different people in different places (and perhaps for different purposes) have happened to undertake studies not too dissimilar for comparison. For theoretical, methodological, and practical reasons, full replication is rarely possible. Nor is formal replication necessarily desirable. The strength of sociological results rarely depends upon the precise accuracy of a single item of data— results are more frequently built up by the analysis and comparison of different kinds of data, from different sources and 'replication' is carried out internally by the comparison of findings from separate analyses as well as by comparison of raw data. This does not of course justify technical sloppiness but, under the particular exigencies of sociological research, it provides the equivalent of checks on reliability and validity. This technique of 'triangulation' (Denzin, 1970) is applicable to different data sources and analyses within a single project but is equally valuable in the mapping of a large issue in which different research questions dictate the use of multiple designs, each of which may yield qualitatively different material not capable of being compared in their raw form.

The full range of sociological methods can readily be studied in textbooks which are many and varied (see Bulmer, 1977; Schwarz and Jacobs, 1979). Instead of listing and summarizing them, I have attempted, in what follows, to exemplify their use in relation to one set of research problems. This has limitations in that even a broad programme of research does not use, and therefore cannot provide examples of, more than a few methodological approaches. I shall therefore concentrate upon the important questions of research design, the use of multiple methodologies and the interpretative problems posed by different kinds of data. I have centred the discussion around the study of policy problems relating to the handicapped, the mentally ill, the chronic sick, and the elderly, a group of patients whom I categorize collectively as 'dependency groups'.

METHODOLOGICAL ISSUES IN THE STUDY OF DEPENDENCY GROUPS

Policy-makers are being increasingly forced to consider what should be the appropriate arrangements for the medical and social care of persons who cannot be cured yet cannot be fully independent. They include mentally and physically handicapped persons, people who are chronically sick to the point of disablement and a proportion of the mentally ill and of the elderly. The crucial policy question is who should bear what degrees of responsibility for various components of care and support and under what circumstances and arrangements? The decision involves social and economic values and the relative welfare of sizeable population groups and is, in the final analysis, a political one. However, the policy problem contains a number of discrete issues, which in the words of the Royal Commission can 'be illuminated with fact'. The alternative to existing arrangements being most widely discussed is that of community care. Spelled out more clearly this might involve any or all of the following: the switching of professional resources from hospital and institutional care to family support, out-patient facilities, and day hospitals and centres; the expansion of support facilities to enable dependent persons to remain in their own homes or those of relatives, involving, in turn, financial and domestic support and professional advice and help to relatives, neighbours, and friends; the initiation and development of neighbourhood support schemes operated on a voluntary basis by local people and organizations, again with the support and material assistance of statutory health and social service authorities and their professional staff. A policy change in the location of responsibility for dependency groups thus raises many questions. I shall restrict myself to those which pose methodological problems, not just for the study of dependency groups but for sociological research in general.

1. Definition of the problem
The perceived need for change derives from a conjunction of trends. Some stem from the services themselves—the pressure on health service resources caused by increased costs, the desire to exploit new but costly techniques of treatment, the restriction on the total budget available in the face of continuing demand, the past inability to shift resources towards dependency groups and occasional outbreaks of public concern at the poor standards of care available in residential institutions for the mentally ill, the mentally retarded, and the elderly. The effect on planning and the implementation of priorities resulting from the creation of a separate and unified system of social services is still unclear but there is an assumption backed by fragmentary evidence that separate administrations and budgets inhibit co-ordinated planning and place barriers on the transfer of clients between appropriate facilities. Other pressures are seen to derive from population and social change external to the services; the absolute and proportionate increase of dependency groups in the population (partially due to improved medical techniques), the increasing age of the elderly and therefore of their family supporters; the increased involvement of women in the workforce; increased geographical and social mobility leading to the break-up of supporting networks of kin and neighbours and an hypothesized decrease in the willingness of family members to accept responsibility for the care of their dependants. Many of these factors are simultaneously constraints on policy change. Any new policy relying for its success on the use of formal or informal resources whose recent withdrawal had created the policy problem might be creating a Canute-like situation.

As a first step in defining the problem and in seeking alternative solutions a historical dimension to research is clearly necessary. Some questions are already covered by existing data and pose no methodological problems—this applies mainly to the facts of demographic change. For most other components, however, the simple demonstration of incontrovertible fact (e.g. increased female involvement in paid work, and increased geographical mobility) still leaves unanswered questions about their implications for the care of dependency groups. Has the increased labour-force participation of women itself reduced their ability to assume responsibility? Alternatively have they accepted continuing responsibility by adapting their other activities, by mobilizing other family resources, or by suffering increasing strain—and have there been counter-acting tendencies in the shape of better housing, better domestic technology, increased living standards, easier travel, the use of telephones, and a greater tendency for duties to be shared by other family members, particularly men? Has change and adaptation to change occurred to the same degree and with similar results across the social spectrum? In all social classes, in urban and rural life? Has affluence protected some against the strains of responsibility or given them access to facilities not enjoyed by others? Very similar questions can be posed in relation to increased geographical and social mobility.

Most difficult methodologically, however, is the assumption that family members have a reduced willingness to care for their own. Such willingness or propensity to care is clearly crucial to any policy of family or community care. Motivation is difficult to establish among the living. Its reconstruction for those now dead or for those who faced responsibility in the past is subject to paucity of contemporary data, to errors of recall, and post-hoc glosses and interpretations which reflect the respondent's current situation and beliefs. Even if sociologists had studied similar issues two decades previously, unless the contrast in responses were sharp, the comparison would present considerable difficulties partly because of the different situations to which informants would be responding and partly because of intervening changes in public attitudes. In the absence of such potentially comparable data we must, however reluctantly, leave out a historical dimension and design a study of present-day willingness.

Study of the service end of the problem would also ideally contain a historical dimension. The problem itself is not a new one and historical study might reveal what past policies had been tried, what success they had achieved and what resistances they had encountered. It would be necessary to seek answers to questions such as the following. How clearly has policy been

articulated over the last 20 years, by what professional, governmental, and other public voices? To what extent have policies
been backed by legislation, regulation, guidance, and resources?
To what extent have changes already occurred, in the numbers
and proportions of dependent persons being cared for by residential, hospital, and community facilities, in the numbers and
types of facilities, in the provision of increased or differently-used
health personnel? What evidence is there that the failure to shift
resources came from other service interests rather than from
organizational inertia in the machinery of planning and its
implementation? Many innovatory schemes of limited and
local coverage have arisen throughout the UK (and other countries) in response to the problem. Have some succeeded better
than others and can anything be learnt from differential success
about the likelihood that larger schemes incorporating elements
of these experiments would succeed in the future?

Evidence would also be valuable on changes in medical
thought and practice towards dependency groups particularly in
relation to medical education and staff recruitment and rewards.
Differences are likely between different levels of the health
system. We might expect not only that nurses, general practitioners, psychiatrists, and geriatricians will differ from surgeons,
gynaecologists, and pathologists, but also that they will differ
from each other in the pressures they feel, the barriers that
constrain their actions, and the solutions they deem possible
and desirable.

One special feature of dependency groups is that they are not
wholly, and perhaps not primarily, the responsibility of the
health service. Action by housing authorities and social services
may delay or prevent the onset of dependency or minimize its
repercussions by identification and referral, by the organization
of community schemes and by use of their own spectrum of
graded facilities. Social security is heavily involved through its
financial support system and, with some categories of the chronic
sick and disabled, so is the Department of Employment. One major
hypothesis states that the intransigence of the problem results
from divided administration, conflicting definitions and ideologies, and the barriers to unified action created by separate

bureaucracies. Internal and comparative study of the health and the social services would clearly be needed to identify potential blockages to planning and practice and possible dangers and opportunities in a revised policy.

In the preceding discussion it has been assumed that the mentally and physically handicapped, the mentally ill, the chronic sick, and the dependent elderly are rendered homogeneous in policy terms by their common possession of dependency status. This is clearly not true and a study of their differences might be revealing of policy requirements. Some are more, some less susceptible to professional skills in medicine and social work; emotional reactions to physical and mental handicap and illness differ and some are seen as more troublesome or less deserving by the general public.

In this review of the ways in which the problem of dependency groups might be defined I have touched upon a number of issues which have wider methodological significance. First, the sociological definition of the problem takes it outside and across established governmental and service boundaries. In the case in hand, our formulation of the problem started from a category of patients/clients but took us into studies of population change, family and community functioning, the needs of various dependency groups, the moral stance of individuals and groups towards need and responsibility, the ideology of professions, the development of policy, the politics of decision-making, the evaluation of social experiment, and the determinants of organizational change and resource distribution. Sociologists often find that their definition of the problem results in a wider sphere of relevance than might be employed by, say, an epidemiologist. There are a number of reasons for this, starting with the sociologists' reluctance to work with conventional and, they would claim, sectional definitions of the problem. C. Wright Mills (1959) is perhaps most eloquent on this point:

Do not allow public issues as they are officially formulated, or troubles as they are privately felt, to determine the problems that you take up for study. . . . Know that many personal troubles cannot be solved merely as troubles, but must be understood in terms of public issues—and in terms of the problems of history-making. Know that the human meaning of public issues must be

The methodology of sociology

revealed by relating them to personal troubles—and to the problems of the individual life. Know that the problems of social science, when adequately formulated, must include both troubles and issues, both biography and history, and the range of their intricate relations.

This reluctance of sociologists to accept conventional definitions is associated with their commitment to an overarching perspective—well illustrated in their preference for a sociology *of* medicine over a sociology *in* medicine; the former giving them the freedom to study the social organization of medicine and its relationship with other institutional spheres, the latter restricting their interests to the social factors associated with disease and illness behaviour. There is also the separate but related issue of the sociologists' attempt to view events from the viewpoint of the individual social actor. Sociologists still take seriously W. I. Thomas' dictum, 'If men define situations as real, they are real in their consequences', and in so doing, they inevitably commit themselves to an open-ended strategy for formulating and defining the problem. I have already provided an extended illustration of this strategy but it can be found in every good piece of sociological research. Restricting my examples to work carried out by my own colleagues in Aberdeen, neither Blaxter (1976) nor Macintyre (1977) could have arrived at their appraisals of the disability and maternity services if they had not started from a sociological formulation of the problem. Rather than describing the services and their problems from the point of view of those responsible for running them, they both chose to study the actual experiences of a cohort of patients. By focusing on the patients rather than the services, they were able to identify many instances of discrepancy between need and provision. Blaxter's study was of particular interest, illustrating the ways in which the patients' own self-definitions were affected by, and in turn affected, the definition used by official agencies. Studying a sample of patients discharged from hospital, and tracing their daunting and often fortuitous pathways, she was able to show the Byzantine complexity of services available to the disabled and chronically sick. Over all, her study provided an eloquent testimony, subsequently used by the Royal Commission on the NHS, of the lack of fit between administrative and clinical categories and the

147

patient's own definition of his condition and eligibility for help.
The second more general point I would want to make relates
specifically to techniques of study. My definition of the problem
of responsibility for dependency groups involves the use of
historical materials, demographic data, administrative statistics,
the content analysis of policy documents and professional statements and curricula, the evaluation of experiments, and the
gathering of data about the attitudes and behaviour of categories
of the population and of policy-makers and practitioners at
different points in the delivery of care. Details of these various
techniques are available in any handbook of sociological method.
The point I wish to emphasize is that the sociologist needs to be
master of many techniques of study, and while he rarely is (for
reasons advanced later), this remains a paramount ideal. Writing
as a sociologist I find it ironic that, for me, the best example of
methodological catholicity and all round competence is provided
in Richard Titmuss' *The Gift Relationship* (1970). Titmuss would
not be formally described as a sociologist, yet his approach to the
study of blood transfusion systems is precisely that which I
advocate for the study of dependency groups. His opening para-
graph exemplifies the wide range of his approach:

The starting point of this book is human blood: the scientific, social, economic
and ethical issues involved in its procurement, processing, distribution, use and
benefit in Britain, the United States, the U.S.S.R., South Africa and other
countries. The study thus examines beliefs, attitudes and values concerning
blood and its possession, inheritance, use and loss in diverse societies, past and
present, and draws on historical, religious and sociological materials. It investi-
gates by a variety of research methods the characteristics of those who give,
supply or sell blood, and analyses in comparative terms blood transfusion and
donor systems and national statistics of supply, demand and distribution
particularly in Britain and the United States. Criteria of social value, cost
efficiency, biological efficacy, safety and purity are applied to public and
private markets in blood and to voluntary and commercial systems of meeting
steeply rising world demands from medicine for blood and blood products.

My third more general point relates to another ideal— that of
the integrated whole. The objectives of each component of a
large design need to be matched to each other so that when the
results are fitted together they supplement each other and provide

more than the sum of their parts. For a comprehensive understanding of policy as it affects dependency groups we need to know whether attitudes match behaviour, whether decision-making at one level is consistent with objectives at other levels, whether co-ordination merely requires administrative tinkering or ideological conversion, etc. I must emphasize that this holistic approach represents an ideal. In practice most policy research in the social sciences is conducted by separate individuals, doing one-off projects, at different times and places, responding to different curiosities and adopting idiosyncratic designs. The resulting task of making applicable sense out of diverse and incomplete material increases immeasurably the element of judgement in applied sociology.

My fourth point relates to scale. A rounded study of the kind I envisage, capable of acting as the basis for policy in a major area of resource expenditure, would be large and expensive Funding, on this scale, is quite exceptional in sociological research. Provision for dependency groups is only one of a handful of medico-social problems which require programme funding on this scale. Ageing is another area in which there is a need for programmatic research. Problems of research funding are probably the main reason for the virtual absence of any longitudinal research. This is a serious omission. Cross-sectional studies can tell us very little about the process of ageing, and they distort our understanding of the elderly population, since they are always based on a sample of survivors. For example, a cross-sectional survey of a sample of male pensioners tells us nothing about the 20 per cent who reach the age of 55 but die before they reach 65, and their absence distorts our understanding of those factors associated with differential survival and psycho-social functioning. Apart from being essential for an understanding of the ageing process itself, longitudinal research designs would also advance our understanding of a range of social phenomena associated with ageing—particularly retirement, bereavement, and impairment.

To return to social responsibility for dependency groups, having outlined a sociological definition of the problem, I now want to go on and describe three further strands in a compre-

149

hensive study. Again, while the details relate to dependency groups, the discussion is intended to illustrate methodological issues common to all broadly based sociological research.

2. Public conceptions of need

The debate about priorities, the shortage of resources and facilities for the chronic sick and the disabled, about cure and care, is conducted within a limited circle of administrators, health and social service professionals, politicians, and pressure groups. It surfaces at election times when politicians trot out the arguments about safeguarding our hospitals, schools and old age pensions, and on those fortunately rare occasions when atrocities and scandals occur in some of our residential institutions. To a large extent, however, the needs of dependency groups are interpreted for us by an articulate group of people involved either in the administration and delivery of care or in pressure groups representing particular groups of clients. It is at least arguable that the political will to shift resources is lacking because the public will is also missing. Unions and employers, potentially among the most powerful arbiters of public policy, concentrate upon the welfare of their own, active and employed members. Family and community care of the dependent, however, touches most people at some point and we have very little knowledge of their priorities or of the extent to which they are concordant with those of professionals. What could we discover about public expectations and about acceptance or denial of responsibility by conducting an enquiry among a representative sample of the population?

It would certainly be relatively easy to design and conduct a survey of attitudes. Such a survey would attempt to elicit attitudes towards different types and degrees of dependency, the forms of support or types of responsibility regarded as appropriate, and who should assume particular types and degrees of responsibility. One part of the interview would need to cover the respondent's own characteristics. Most of these characteristics could be simply described as socio-demographic facts—age, sex, marital status, and occupation. They would be used to check the homogeneity of responses and the sources of variations in attitudes and opinion.

We would also want to identify the respondent's ideological stance towards state versus family forms of provision in order to distinguish between responses indicative of a general orientation and those relating specifically to dependency and types of support. The main part of the interview would need to cover the question of *who* would assume *what degrees of responsibility* with *what types of support* and how responsibility and support should vary according to the nature and degree of the dependant's condition, his social circumstances, and the availability and resources of the family. Under *who* it would be necessary to cover the range of possibilities from the individual himself, his family members, neighbours and voluntary organization to the medical, nursing, and social services and the social security system. Degrees of responsibility would refer to such alternatives as personal or shared, discretionary or mandatory, temporary or permanent, home-based or institutional arrangements. And forms of support would need to refer to the various possibilities of impersonal support (e.g. money, housing, transport, meals, and physical aids) and of personal support (e.g. personal care, domestic help, advice and counselling, nursing and medical care, help with employment, and family problems etc.).

We do not have such information about public attitudes towards these crucial issues of public policy. The technical exercise of eliciting valid responses would be difficult, but assuming it would be possible, what would be the status of such information? Variations in awareness of existing provision and of the responsibilities already assumed by individuals, families and organizations would undoubtedly make interpretation difficult. Some would be speaking from personal experience, and the particular experiences on which their attitudes and opinions were based would be highly variable. Others, without such personal experience, would be speaking from a general moral viewpoint culled from many sources. All respondents, however, would be responding to hypothetical questions about hypothetical situations. Responses given in the comparative tranquillity of a formal interview, whilst drawing upon and reflecting a general position or strategy (which itself is important) are not responses to actual situations. They may, for many reasons, be misleading guides to behaviour. If the respondent is aware that, from a moral or professional standpoint, there are 'right' or 'proper' or expected' responses, he/she may prefer to display them rather than give a personal and perhaps a deviant reaction. This is a constant and acknowledged defect in questionnaire work. In an interview situation respondents are not subject to the constraints engendered by personal accountability for making decisions, they do not have to balance benefits in one area against costs in another, neither do they have to live with the consequences. Moreover, in real life situations a clear-cut choice rarely occurs 'in vacuo'. More frequently a situation develops gradually; minor events and decisions unfold over time and themselves become factors in later events and decisions. The ultimate course of action is therefore best seen as a final, or possibly final, stage in a succession of decisions, each taken in uncertainty about the real situation. Any specific situation is also surrounded by contingencies which cannot be fully predicted or imagined. Individuals, for example, frequently need to act jointly with others whose own responses may be unpredictable; social and economic factors (housing, work, and money) are changeable; the full knowledge about the dependent person's circumstances will consist of complex, even contradictory features and uncertainties; administrative and health or social service facts may be unknown or incorrectly understood. Given these unrealities of the interview, it is unlikely that respondents' answers would be reliable predictors of their own behaviour when faced with the problem of caring for, or arranging for the care of, a dependent person.

This does not necessarily invalidate the results as indicators of the possible behaviour of the population as a whole. Demographers, asking questions about family intentions, have found that, while there is a poor correlation between stated intention and ultimate family size for individuals the aggregated intentions of individuals are predictive of trends in family size for the whole population. The reasons for this paradox are complex, but it is likely that individual departures from intention offset each other and that the total response is indicative of a generally prevalent intention. Thus, it is possible that the results of a survey of the opinions of dependent persons and their families, whilst a poor guide to individual behaviour, might be indicative of a moral climate relevant to public policy.

Though subject to some of the defects discussed above, differences between groups and differences in attitudes towards particular measures may provide useful policy guides. Some support measures, and some types of responsibility might be seen as more acceptable than others. Variations between age and sex groups, between those who have or have not had personal experience of dependency, between those more or less likely to assume the burden of care, might permit some inferential interpretation or lead to hypotheses which could be tested in other ways. Responses to questions about particular disabling conditions might reveal popular distinctions between them.

If, however, we require 'hard data' based on real-life confrontations, rather than responses to hypothetical situations, additional methodological approaches are necessary. One type of approach which has gained ground in recent years is described below.

3. Client-services interaction

This strategy is based upon the premise that social beings act in response to their perception of the complex contingencies surrounding events and not merely to the events themselves. The general orientations identified in an attitudinal survey might affect both perceptions and behaviour, but the translation of general orientations into concrete action will also depend upon particularities—the preceding relationship of the dependent to his family members, friends and neighbours, their other duties, involvements and expectations, the exigencies of housing, transport, money and time, informal help and advice from kin and friends, the definitions, diagnoses, prognoses and options offered by doctors, social workers, and other service-providers, the availability and accessibility of statutory or voluntary facilities, the frustrations experienced through bottlenecks and blockages in services, etc. The research strategy involves taking all such contingencies into account by following the patient/client through his experiences from early identification of the problem, observing events as they unfold and at each stage obtaining not only the clients' own account but also those from informal and formal advisers, helpers, and service providers involved in the process. Various accounts from different participants in the same process are thus compiled, each dealing with definitions of the problem, options perceived, options rejected, barriers encountered, and actions taken. In carrying out such field work, the sociologist would have a list of research questions (i.e. issues integral to the problem) and of topics related to these research questions, but the interviews would be informal, centred around the particular case, and neither structured nor standardized.

This research strategy has advantages and costs. On the credit side, it deals with real situations with all their idiosyncratic features, and records what happens rather than what should or might happen. The case imposes its own structure upon the investigator and is therefore less likely than a pre-structured survey to produce only what the investigator built in from the beginning. The final compilation of the case-history will have a framework of events, but the content will consist of the perception of events and relationships as perceived by the participants. It thus meets the stringent conditions of the qualitative sociologist quoted earlier that 'social meanings (which direct behaviour) do not inhere in activities, institutions or social objectives themselves. Rather, meanings are conferred upon social events by interacting individuals. . . .'

On the debit side it is time-consuming and expensive because the field worker is not a paid interviewer but a professional sociologist who alone is capable of capitalizing upon the unstructured situation. This means that, for a given budget, the number of cases studied will be many fewer than the number of persons interviewed in a social survey (against this, the case-history contains repeated interviews with a range of persons performing different roles). In free interview situations thousands of words are spoken, accompanied by hesitations, qualifications, and interruptions. The same sequence of remarks would not occur with a different interviewer. Replication is not possible because the persons and events are peculiar to one place and time. Most sociologists would wish to tape these inter-actions so that the material can be studied at leisure and analysed in different ways.

The methodology of sociology

Apart from the sheer mass of taped and typed material, the sociologist is faced with the difficult task of abstracting what is relevant and this leaves the approach open to criticisms of subjectivity and selective reporting. Whilst techniques and rules of analysis are available they cannot be rigidly applied to such spontaneously generated data and whilst the taped and typed material can be retained for external inspection (if rules of confidentiality can be maintained) it is unrealistic to expect that re-analysis by other persons will occur.

The likelihood of subjective bias is reduced if other material can be placed alongside—demographic and documentary sources, the results of parallel social surveys of a larger population, observation in clinics and institutions, etc. Thus, by bringing to bear different types of data on a common problem, a form of triangulation occurs within this interactionist strategy in that the material does not consist of a single account but of accounts by different participants whose views must be compared, even if they cannot be reconciled (for an example of this strategy see Macintyre, 1977).

Other qualitative strategies, some more restrictive on the research worker's right to interpret events which he has not personally observed, would be advocated by different schools of sociological thought. Their common feature, however, is the attempt to let the situation and the participants speak for themselves rather than for the sociologist to impose meanings derived from preconceptions.

4. Professional definitions and decision-making

Policy is concerned with the identification and meeting of need. What I have described as *the moral climate of need*, a distillation of public views, might emerge from a survey of public opinion. Equally, the practising definitions of need employed by patients and their families might emerge from a client/service interaction study. Policy, however, is implemented by administrators and professionals, and their definitions of need are based on different criteria (for a discussion of the concept of need see Smith, 1980.) Crudely stated the professional's definition responds to the question, 'Does this person have needs amenable to my skills?' Moral and professional need are obviously related. Increasing

155

sensitivity to human welfare widens the legitimate scope of professional intervention from death to suffering and discomfort while, simultaneously, technological advance enhances professional skills to encompass a greater range of problems. The extent of concordance/discordance in relation to particular categories of patients is not known. Administrators, deploying scarce resources and manpower to meet an infinitely expandable volume of problems also have to develop operational criteria for acceptance or refusal of service. Their definition must primarily respond to the question 'Do we have resources to meet this category of moral or professional need?' It is the discordance between these different definitions which from time to time erupts into professional or public acrimony and into administrative frustration (and structural reorganization?).

Some conception of professional need would, as I have suggested, be revealed by the client/inter-actionist strategy, but it would be limited to the cases and practitioners involved. A fuller picture would emerge from an adaptation of the attitude and opinion survey of the general public. Its form would be different (professionals react less co-operatively to structured interviews with paid interviewers) and its penetration deeper. Service professionals are likely to have encountered dependency situations frequently as part of their normal working lives and they will have a battery of typical cases from which they can draw inferences and conclusions; their knowledge of the relevant machinery will be greater and they will be familiar with the constraints upon ideal practice. They may well have evolved their own policies and strategies for dealing, not only with clients but also with policy guidelines, collegial practices, and administrative procedures. They are likely to have opinions about desired shifts of resources within and between the health and social services. Interview and analysis would therefore have to be adapted accordingly.

Professional practice and policy implementation are intertwined. I suggested in chapter 5 that policy in action is composed of its interpretation by professional and administrative staff. New policy, and particularly the machinery for its implementation, for 'making priorities stick' in the words of the Royal Commission on the NHS, must therefore take account of the ideologies and motivations of established medicine, nursing, and administration (some sociologists would extend this to the practices of reception-ists in GP surgeries, emergency departments, and social work departments—Smith, 1980). One example of a sociological approach to decision-making as it relates to priorities was de-scribed in chapter 6—Hunter's case study in two Area Health Boards of the use of Development Funds. This approach is useful because it reveals the position taken by interested parties at the point when decisions have to be made about a shift of resources between sectors. It is capable of application to many other cir-cumstances. When budgets are restricted or reduced and when socio-economic changes highlight latent problems, existing interests are threatened and orientations previously taken for granted need defence. The closing or rationalization of hospitals, the transfer of maternity units to geriatric use, the economic con-centration of specialist services in a few centres, and the with-drawal of resources from other centres are often accompanied by protest and negotiation in which the issues are exposed. Taylor's (1977) study of the proposal to withdraw the sole local practitioner from an Orcadian island in the interests of resource rationalization provides an interesting example of the way in which a local issue can be used to expose underlying social and service ideologies. He summarized the outcome of his ethnographic case study as follows:

The re-construction of a controversy in the local system reveals the ways in which these different [professional, managerial and lay] groups formulate and pursue their interests both within and out of the formal structure. Professional-lay and managerial-professional conflicts provide the central themes and the paper is ultimately concerned with the question, *'who defines health needs?'*

Data collection methods were far removed from those of the formally structured survey:

Over the course of my 12 month stay, I attended most meetings of the Area Health Board, the Local Health Council, and the Area Medical and Nursing Advisory Committees. I interviewed administrators and professionals and was able to observe many of them in action. Not having my own room I spent a lot of time in Health Board and hospital offices and in doctors' surgeries and sitting rooms. I lingered over Health Centre tea and coffee breaks, and loitered in hospital corridors and car parks. Throughout, I asked questions and listened to answers. On the basis of these activities, which I call field work, I began to formulate a more abstract conception of the local health system.

What emerged therefore was Taylor's own formulation of how needs were defined and how conflicting priorities emerged in practice, but it was based on the participants' views and actions. The internal workings of a system are not so visible in the more complex health systems of large urban authorities but methods have and are being developed. The Royal Commission on the NHS commissioned several sets of case studies (Kogan, 1978; Barnard, Lee and Reynolds, 1977; Battye, Burdett and Smith, 1977). The latter two reports explore the feasibility of 'retrospective decision-tracking' and the adequacy of recorded material for the reconstruction of both events and processes. Barnard et al stress the necessity of a triangulation approach insisting on at least four key sources (minutes, agenda papers, files, and interviews with key witnesses) and note that, 'If the researcher is not allowed access to all (four) sources the outcome will be a very partial and incomplete picture of the way in which decisions have been made'.

There are limitations to this research strategy. Free access is clearly essential and has to be built upon trust, a requirement which is intrinsically difficult if the analysis is likely to uncover uncomfortable events. Restriction of the method to decisions taken omits many interesting non-issues and non-decisions. In prospective work it is not easy to identify a problem and to be in position to observe its emergence; and if it is difficult to know when a case begins, it is also difficult to know when it should end because implementation is often a long-drawn-out process. As with methods discussed earlier the process of analysis is partially hidden and this can only be overcome by lengthy presentation of negative as well as positive leads (perhaps this is one reason why sociology tends to produce a large number of full-length books rather than articles). And there is the constant problem of how far results can be generalized beyond the particular issue and its time and place.

Using one theme, the location of responsibility for dependency groups, I have only been able to illustrate a few methodological approaches. My main point has been that sociological study faces intrinsic theoretical and methodological problems because the events which can be incontrovertibly regarded as facts are few, and they have little explanatory power. Getting behind the facts into the processes by which they are created takes sociologists into the world of social meanings which, in turn, leaves them vulnerable to charges of subjectivity. Aware of the vulnerability of their findings, they have developed batteries of theory, methodology and techniques which, as is common in the scientific world, often take the form of schools of thought so bitterly opposed that exponents dislike their closest professional colleagues more than their enemies. One recent, sympathetic, highly sophisticated (and readable) exposition of qualitative sociology (Schwartz and Jacobs, 1979) concluded: 'We see no optimistic signs that qualitative sociology has unearthed the tools that will eventually make a science of society possible, be that science of the phenomenological, ethnomethodological or symbolic interactionist variety. However, this would not exclude the possibility of achieving sociological understanding'. In the pursuit of understanding in the field of health and medicine, and as an interim recipe, I have advocated a multi-faceted approach involving both quantitative and qualitative methodologies in which from an initial definition of the problem, an attack is developed using designs and techniques most appropriate to each component issue. Putting the pieces together raises the contradictions and biases intrinsic to each approach and provides a check on the presuppositions, but not the integrity of the researcher. It is, however, an expensive strategy in terms of current sociological funding and requires the planned co-operative effort of a team of research workers who have already become familiar with the field and can expect to pursue their work together on a long-term basis. In the next chapter I question whether the conditions of production capable of generating research of this kind and quality yet exist outside a few special situations.

8

The contribution and current problems of medical sociology

When the newly-formed British Sociological Association held its first annual conference in the early 1950s, one of its three sections was devoted to the study of health. Of the six speakers, four were medical doctors, one was a medical administrator, and only one a sociologist. In 1956 the five British 'sociologists' working full-time on problems of health and medicine began a series of meetings on social class and disease and, of these five, three had trained as anthropologists and two as economists. Their patrons, Dugald Baird, John Brotherston, Aubrey Lewis, and Jerry Morris, were innovative clinicians and epidemiologists who had identified a dimension in their work which went beyond epidemiology and seemed to require the study of patients as social beings. As one of those five, I did not think of myself as a medical sociologist, or even as a sociologist, but as an ex-economist and town planner, interested in class and poverty, temporarily located in a medical milieu. My research problems had sprung directly out of medical practice and been formulated by medical scientists and my investigative techniques were primarily epidemiological. Writing later (Illsley, 1975) about the development of medical sociology as a discipline, I commented:

What perhaps primarily distinguished this from later phases in the development of medical sociology was the acceptance of medical formulations of the problem using medical models and definitions of disease, and the relative absence of studies of the medical profession, medical services, diagnostic and treatment procedures, and of outcome in social terms. Studies of the individual and of processes contributing to illness, but external to medical institutions were non-threatening to the medical profession at this tentative stage of cross-disciplinary co-operation. It is perhaps worth noting that, at this period, much empirical sociological work in other fields was equally naive and limited in scope, and that the theoretical perspectives now most commonly used in medical sociology were either unknown to, ignored by, or condemned by, orthodox sociology.

The position today is very different. General sociology has been strengthened by the passage of time, by its quite spectacular growth in the Universities during the 1960s, by the maturing of its new entrants in the subsequent decade, and by its increased involvement in many sectors of the economy and government. Medical sociology has also grown in the number of its practitioners, its theoretical and methodological sophistication, and its working familiarity with medicine and the operation of the health services. Whereas I could earlier describe medical sociology as 'something of a pariah in orthodox sociology' it has now become one of the strongest sectors of sociology. The small group of five which met in 1956 has grown into an annual meeting attended by up to 250 participants, who have their own journal, *Sociology of Health and Illness*, and who contribute widely to medical and sociological journals in the UK and abroad. The latest Register of research and teaching in medical sociology (Arber, 1978) lists 270 names and they by no means include the full complement of sociologists contributing to the topic. The subject is now taught with varying degrees of serious commitment in most medical schools, colleges of nursing, and health visitor training schools in the UK. In a diverse subject area it is difficult to produce a classification of research topics which adequately reflects the substantive and methodological spread of a discipline, but the classification adopted in the Register gives a reasonable indication of the volume and distribution of research themes.

The subject list reveals not merely growth in the volume of research compared with previous decades but important changes of emphasis. Sociology is a reflexive discipline in that its concerns mirror those of the society in which it is located. That partially explains the heavy concentration upon disability, chronic sickness and rehabilitation, the elderly, alcoholism and drug abuse, mental illness, and behaviour disturbances. It may also reflect selective funding, and hence the concerns of the Health Departments through the Chief Scientist Organizations. In most fields the bulk of research deals with the work of health professionals in contact with patients, the relationship of administrative procedures or modes of diagnosis and treatment to the needs of patients, and the impact of particular illnesses and their treatment

Subject	Current research projects
Health beliefs and behaviour; health education	44
Illness behaviour and self-medication	22
The health professions	53
Patient-practitioner communication	8
Hospital-based studies	23
General practitioner-based studies	32
The organization of health care; health planning and health consumers	19
Social epidemiology	29
Disability, chronic sickness, and rehabilitation	60
The elderly; dying	31
Family planning, including abortion	20
Pregnancy and childbirth	24
Child health care	34
Mental illness and behaviour disturbances	28
Alcoholism and drug dependence	17
Suicide and attempted suicide	6
Health behaviour and health care in the Third World	11
Other	24

upon the social lives of patients. It therefore differs sharply from earlier work which concentrated upon the individual and the aetiology of disease, and which tended to take medicine and its procedures for granted. This emphasis upon professionals and their work is not specific to the medical area but reflects a more general sociological trend over the last 20 years to regard the operation of agencies and their staff as problematic—many similar studies have examined social service agencies and social workers, education and teachers, the law and the police. Whatever its origins, it indicates a deeper familiarity with the daily workings of medicine and the health services and adds up to a constant stream of evaluative work with the sociologist exploring and representing the interests of the consumer. By contrast, medical sociologists have been doing very little research, at the policy and system level, on health planning and the organization of health care. This again may reflect selective funding from the Health Departments and difficulties of access for detailed observational inter-actionist work on the policy and planning process.

The contribution and current problems of medical sociology

Throughout earlier chapters I have identified two gaps in knowledge fundamental to our understanding of health and illness and to the formulation and development of health and social policy. I take the opportunity in these conclusions to elaborate upon them.

SOCIAL STRUCTURE AND HEALTH-RELATED BEHAVIOUR

We can demonstrate the association between death, disease, and social factors and have been able to do so throughout the century. The disease and death side of the equation has been spelled out with increasing detail and certainty throughout these years, diseases being progressively differentiated and related on the one hand to physiological, biochemical, and neurological processes and on the other to techniques of diagnosis and treatment. Colin Dollery's earlier Rock Carling monograph illustrated the enormously detailed cumulative development by which, in field after field, a crude art was transformed into a very advanced technological science. By contrast, the other side of the equation, 'social factors', remains conceptually and empirically under-developed. We have, of course, learnt a lot about social class, work, education, marriage, family, and other major social institutions; we have conceptually refined and empirically documented such life-stage and behavioural phenomena as upbringing, adolescence, or old age, as anomie, deviance and socialization. We have not however, developed them as *categories for use*. Take for example, the known and large gap in death rates of persons in Social Class V in East Anglia and North West England. We do know, and can demonstrate through census-type statistics, that they represent a different array of occupations; but even if we take a particular and precise occupational category, the differences remain. By drawing on many other sources of aggregated data we could draw up, as Townsend (1979) has done for poverty, a profile of some typical characteristics of Social Class V (but not for precise occupations) in respect of average income and expenditure, dietary patterns, social security receipts, etc. Variations in life-styles, even within a class or occupation, are large, as also are death rates and particularly death rates from particular diseases.

163

It is therefore quite impossible, from available sources, to relate detailed life-styles to particular diseases or even to early death. Ideally the investigative process should be reversed—instead of identifying Class and building up typical or average characteristics around it, we should be starting from life-styles and differentiating groups who share common environments and behavioural styles, so that internally homogeneous groups can be compared in respect of a variety of outcomes. I occasionally compare the use of social classification to the physician's use of thermometer. It may confirm the existence of certain kinds of disturbance, but not others, and it gives only the haziest clue about what to do next. The data, however, are so easy to collect and manipulate, so comforting in their stability of associations with mortality, that no urgency has been felt to develop better diagnostic aids. On a national scale the only social factors available for cross-tabulation against death and disease are crude categories of this kind—class, marital status, age, and region of residence. Our nearest approximations to the natural life-history of populations is provided by a few longitudinal studies of national samples of children compiled from medical and administrative statistics and supplemented by periodic surveys using tests, scales, and questionnaire material. Respondents in these studies are spread across the UK to obtain a representative national sample, and while this is quite justifiable for certain research purposes, it does mean that each one is snatched from his social environment of family and friends and from his inter-actions with local culture and institutions. The insights possible from observational approaches are inevitably sacrificed. So also is our ability to match variations in health and disease between regions and communities with detailed knowledge of the experience of life for sub-sections of the population of those regions and communities.

My suggestion is that for a selection of communities across the UK we need in-depth and continuing descriptive studies using the whole range of sociological approaches to document the demographic, social, and economic 'facts' about living conditions and working lives and family structure, descriptive accounts of personal and social habits, and behaviour potentially relevant to health and health-behaviour, and of coping styles and orientations towards problems of living together, with the belief systems and experience on which they are seen to be based. Within these contexts we would need to construct life-histories, to identify the conditions and experience which produce divergence and convergence in pathways over the life-cycle because it is such experience, objective and subjective, which, in the final analysis, determines health beliefs, health-related behaviour and health outcomes. The mere compilation of data archives, however, is a dull business unlikely to engage the commitment of lively minds. Such archives tend to generate their own needs and to become progressively irrelevant over time unless they constantly are used, refined and modified by the asking of questions—a phenomenon often described by my epidemiological mentor, Angus Thomson, as 'huge hunks of data untouched by human thought'. It is the simultaneous asking of questions derived either from theory or from practical problems which transforms such bodies of inert data into sources of ideas and material for the testing of ideas. My plea therefore is not for data archives, but for the continuous and cumulative exploration of broad themes, by teams of workers diverse in skills and perspectives, under conditions which foster the long-term development of fundamental knowledge and its exploitation. It is based on the axiom that the conditions of production determine the nature of the product. Unless production is organized to facilitate stability and cumulation we will continue to lack the information base on the structure and process of social life which is needed to complement the minutely observed and analysed phenomena of human biology, biochemistry, and natural ecology.

POLICY AND ITS IMPLEMENTATION

Sociologists in many countries and throughout the UK have worked intensively for the last 10–15 years on the health professions, and have studied their modus operandi and their interaction with patients in a variety of clinical settings. It has proved valuable in forging links between sociologists and health professionals across the country and in introducing sociologists to the empirical study of health and medicine as opposed to the abstract theorizing which characterized the earlier phases of the discipline. Sociologists wanting to do empirical work have always found local opportunities to work with service providers at the coal-face, and this is likely to continue. Such settings provide excellent conditions for pursuing the inter-actionist, ethnomethodological and phenomenological research favoured by the current cohort of sociologists. This type of research also fits with the self-image of many sociologists who see themselves as friends of the people in their unequal relationship with bureaucrats and professionals, and as interpreters of their mute desires.

This concentration on the point at which the service is delivered and on the providers of service has been accompanied, however, by the relative neglect not only of those structural conditions which give rise to patients and their problems, but also of the general health system within which professionals work and which, in turn, influences the nature and distribution of services. I have described above the directions of research needed to correct one imbalance. The second imbalance refers to informal and formal decision-making at each layer of the health system from the point of delivery through the administrative structure to the development of policy in the health and social services Departments of government. Clarification of this obscure area requires the same multiple methodologies already applied to the study of health services at the field level. It is inhibited by the political nature of decision-making and the sensitivity of individuals and organizations to external criticism and hence by restriction of access to the daily processes of policy formulation, decision-making, and evaluation. The designation of government Departments as research customers under the Rothschild reorganization opened up the lower-level working of the health services to research workers. It raises, however, in a new form the old question *Quis custodiet custodes?* Given its still-controversial reputation and its self-styled status as a critical discipline sociology is likely to be a late entrant to policy circles, an 'also ran' by comparison with the management consultants and organizational experts.

My main suggestion for opening up policy and its implementation to research and to public discussion has been the establishment of an independent policy/health services evaluation programme with official support and a direct line to political power. Sociologists, however, could do more in this field if they were better organized for applied research.

PROBLEMS IN THE ORGANIZATION OF
MEDICAL SOCIOLOGICAL RESEARCH

Medicine is both a scientific discipline and a practising profession. Its practitioners are spread across the country, performing their professional tasks in thousands of GP surgeries, clinics, and health centres and in stronger concentrations in general practitioner and district hospitals. Its major establishments, and particularly those in University medical schools, have clinical departments in touch with the practice of medicine and access to research facilities and research staff geared towards the production of knowledge relevant to practice. For each clinical service the practice of the profession provides a focus for the identification of problems, a setting for their investigation, and manpower to undertake research. At the national level, the Chief Scientist's Organizations, the MRC, the NHS and the voluntary foundations provide funds and manpower to lead and to supplement research effort across the country. It all adds up to a formidable research enterprise focused upon the production of knowledge and its application.

Sociology has no practice. It is heavily concentrated upon the Universities and other institutions of higher education, and most members of the discipline are professors, readers, and lecturers who see their primary responsibility as teaching. University teaching departments recruit their staff in order to give teaching coverage across the wide range of sociological interests—sociological theory and methodology, and the various specialties dealing with aspects of societal life—work and industry, population and family, the law, deviance and crime, education and knowledge, religion, art and leisure, political structure, social stratification, urban and rural life, planning, the professions, race relations, etc., etc. Among this wide range of specialist areas the sociology of health and illness is a recent entrant. Few departments are large, and whilst there is a tendency for them to specialize, given the needs of curriculum coverage, the scope for specialist concentration of teaching staff is limited. Many teaching staff list a range of specialist interest in their curricula vitae, but these are largely teaching interests, and because research is a secondary activity for most staff, they cannot easily undertake empirical research in more than one area. It is therefore not unusual for a specialist in a topic to be the only departmental specialist in that topic—an isolation sometimes reinforced by a lecturer's perceived need to emphasize his departmental identity.

One common result of such widely-spread interests is that, apart from teaching activities, the main common denominator is a shared interest in sociology at its most abstract levels, those of theory and methodology, and in the latter case not so much the methodology of research as that of the interpretative qualities of different kinds of data. A substantial body of research is therefore based on re-interpretation or synthesis of previous work and the clarification of concepts. This type of research can be fitted into the exigencies of a teaching timetable, rarely involving first hand collection of data from the external world, yet able to provide the basis for long-range debates across the sociological community in professional journals and monographs.

The restricted numerical possibilities for collaborative research within the Department and the superior call of teaching responsibilities manifest themselves in other ways. Departmental meetings focus on joint teaching concerns and Faculty meetings deal almost exclusively with curricular and the administration of teaching. Many departmental heads, partly as a matter of principle, do not extend their leadership and administration to the promotion of departmental research programmes. Research in sociology, as in some other social sciences and in the arts, is frequently seen as a personal activity springing from a man with an idea and pursued either single-handed, with a post-graduate student, or a research assistant. Within this context, the notion of 'research initiatives' is somewhat alien. The Social Science Research Council recently attempted to stimulate major new programmes of research by identifying important and neglected areas, often but not always of policy concern, in which work might be encouraged or commissioned. This research initiative was received with some suspicion

168

by University sociologists and their professional association. The general feeling was that Committee research initiatives could only lead to dull, policy-dominated research and, at the same time, constitute a potential threat to ideas spontaneously generated by individual sociologists.

Within sociology (as within other social sciences to greater or lesser degrees) a major research output derives from the work of postgraduate, and particularly PhD students. The unhappiness caused by cut-backs in postgraduate studentships reflects the importance of postgraduate research to academic departments and student supervisors, who can vicariously promote their research ideas and conduct their personal research through the medium of postgraduate teaching and the preparation of PhD dissertations. Whilst some students are caught up in the theoretical development of ideas the majority have time for, and do undertake, empirical work. The average length of time taken to complete a PhD is approximately five years (not unusual in the arts and social sciences) and the data and ideas generated at this period are usually exploited over a further period, forming the intellectual basis for individual's early professional career.

The PhD is becoming an essential pre-requisite to a research career. I share the growing doubt about the value of the PhD experience as a training ground for research competence. Taken over from an earlier arts-based tradition it typically requires the completion of an original piece of research under the supervision of a tutor-lecturer. Some university departments now require a preparatory period in which the postgraduate is either taught or exposed to advanced theoretical and methodological thought, or, more rarely, required to learn and practise a range of methodological approaches before choosing and embarking upon his PhD research. Too frequently, however, a student moves straight into his PhD training with minimal methodological training and under the supervision of a tutor committed to a particular theoretical/methodological model of research. In these conditions he identifies a research problem, develops his design and conducts his research on a single project, of his own choosing, which may not give him experience outside a very limited frame of reference. At the end of 3, 4, 5, or 6 years he produces a book-length report, to be judged on its original contribution to his chosen field. I do not question its value as an intellectual experience. Its value, however, as a preparation for a research career, particularly outside the strictly academic world, is questionable. There he may be required to tackle research issues, not of his own choosing, requiring a range of methodologies, and involving collaborative work not only with colleagues of a different theoretical persuasion but also with colleagues outside his own discipline. He may also be required to design and complete his work in much shorter periods and to direct it to different audiences with objectives more focused upon applications than upon the intellectual development of the discipline. My own reading of research needs in medical sociology (and indeed other fields where sociology is applied to aspects of social life and organization) is that it requires more research workers aware of, sympathetic to, and able to use selectively a wide range of theory and methodology. They need to build up co-operatively with sociologists and colleagues from other disciplines a comprehensive body of knowledge focused upon problems pertinent to health and medicine and identified through contact with the health system, its clients, and practitioners. The PhD tradition had the tendency to encourage individualistic modes of work, motivated by professional sociological concerns, on problems relevant to the individual's ideological position and suitable for study by one person over a three-year period.

The most urgent need, however, is for a structure of research careers and for stable bases in which to pursue those careers. I have suggested that future research effort should be devoted to building up systematically and comprehensively over time a deeper knowledge and understanding of certain major areas (life-styles, life-cycles, health beliefs, and the formulation and implementation of major policy issues) and the development of techniques for the continuous evaluation of major services. My list was not meant to be exhaustive because my personal knowledge and interests are themselves limited by experience. I have however suggested other areas of relative neglect such as mental retardation and the problems of dependency groups, approaches to health education and health promotion, and problems stemming from the division of labour. I have touched little upon the area of mental illness or of alcohol-related behaviour although I am conscious of the urgent research needs of these fields. These are all areas of social behaviour and socially-organized care to which sociological skills are relevant. Sociologists are working on all these issues and have opened up many fields for further in-depth study. Spontaneous contributions from individual research workers, lecturers, and postgraduate students will continue to produce fresh ideas but the present need is for programmatic studies. This would entail the mapping of a field and its continuous exploration through a series of related and end-on studies similar for example, to the research programme on dependency groups which I described in chapter 7 to illustrate some aspects of sociological methodology. That description, however, fell far short of essential requirements because it did not mention the need for concurrent methodological development and for the exploitation of findings at subsequent stages. There are a few good examples of such work in the U.K. Perhaps the outstanding example is that of George Brown's work on depression and life-events which is now bringing acknowledged results after many years of collaborative work with psychiatrists, the patient development of aetiological theories, painstaking attention to methodological problems and techniques of data collection, the piloting and testing of methods, and the replication of research in carefully chosen communities. The long-term study of reproduction by the MRC Medical Sociology Unit in Aberdeen, to which I have referred several times in this volume, is also exceptional for its organizational stability, its close association with clinical departments, its compilation of data over a generation of childbearing, and its responsiveness to newly emerging issues. The Department of Nursing Studies in Edinburgh with its associated SHHD Research Unit, staffed mainly by nurses but employing sociological perspectives and methods, has made a unique contribution in its shorter history. There are other good examples in the work carried out by smaller teams centred on Margot Jefferys, Ann Cartwright, and Margaret Stacey. Some of these groups have led, or are leading, a project-by-project existence ill-suited to the pursuit of programmatic studies and the retention of committed staff. In the country as a whole there can only be half-a-dozen groups employing five or more medical sociologists and some of these are heavily dependent on chance funding.

Most full-time research workers in medical sociology are employed on short-term contracts, mainly in sociology teaching departments. Their entry is dependent on the sponsorship of established staff, their near-future upon the possibility of another research grant and their long-term future in medical sociological research is unpredictable. The unco-ordinated funding policies of the Research Councils, Chief Scientist Organizations and private foundations give the appearance of choice and freedom from domination by a single paymaster, but they cannot produce the purposeful development or application of knowledge. Instead they result in the continuous recruitment of young staff with little or no research experience or contact with the health system, a high rate of unfinished work as individuals depart for more secure futures, a loss of experienced staff, and short-term projects and programmes which are all parts and no body.

These critical observations have relevance well beyond medical sociology, sociology, or even the social sciences. One major side-effect, however, has particular implications for health and medicine. If medical sociology is to do more than add another dimension to sociology, its work must be seen as relevant to the interests of administrators and professionals in the health and social services, and its findings must be transmitted to them in a form which can be readily understood. Curiosity-research (isn't it interesting that . . .) will continue to flow; the system is set up to produce it. So also will research ending up with the phrase 'more research is needed . . .'. It may also be true that most research has impact only by slowly and imperceptibly changing the information base and perspectives through which actions are decided. Sometime, however, I would like to explore the hypothesis that the chances of implementation are strengthened if the research worker identifies his problems out of intimate knowledge of the field and its practitioners and is in sufficient and frequent contact to disseminate his findings in personal discussions with those responsible for implementation. Most medical staff, for example, will rarely read a sociology journal and I have noted (impressionistically) that their knowledge of medical sociology comes largely through their personal contacts with sociologists. This makes it important to retain a body of sociological staff, who through their previous work, have established working relationships with the services. Current methods of organizing research do not meet this requirement.

What can, and what should, be done? On the one hand we need a continuous output of medical-sociological research generated within sociology and feeding back into its parent discipline. From such a source would come the synthesis of medical sociology with other applied areas, the developments and shifts in paradigms characteristic of any lively science and the independent viewpoints engendered by distancing and by contemplative thought. This is the traditional function of the Universities and considering the prominence of medical sociology within general sociology I have no doubts about its continuance.

Additionally, however, we need a very considerable body of planned programmatic research carried out by groups of research workers who have a commitment to issues in the health field and to the operation of the health services. Favourable circumstances may spontaneously occur within the University framework when a capable and motivated research worker is able to make internal arrangements for a separately administered centre and to attract external research funds. The combination of satisfactory internal and external possibilities is not easy to achieve. Internally the major barrier is the lack of a career structure for research workers comparable with that for University teaching staff. Despite the fact that the UGC contribution to Universities contains an element of research money and that 'in 1977–8 contract research staff constituted 19 per cent of all academic staff employed in Universities' (Salter, 1980) no arrangements have been made, and virtually no attempts made, to incorporate research staff into a career structure which would give them stability beyond the term of their two- or three-year research grant. The arguments justifying this situation, particularly those relating to dual-financing, are and have been familiar to research staff for many years. They are weakened by other features of the Universities' relationships with research staff. Salter comments:

The contribution and current problems of medical sociology

The marginality of research staff is emphasised, gallingly so, by the fact that they do not have parity of status with teaching staff. This is manifested in the absence of rights normally enjoyed by teaching staff: they are frequently denied committee membership, do not have access to internal university research funds, and are not allowed to initiate and be responsible for research projects.

Salter is pessimistic about the capability or willingness of Universities to adapt to the changed status of research and I share his pessimism. They should not be central to immediate plans for the further development of medical sociology.

The Royal Commission on the NHS expressed the need for an Institute for Health Services Research independent of the Government. I suggested a rather different mechanism for the encouragement of evaluation and the opening of public discussion. Neither solution is appropriate for the general development of medical sociology which must have centres across the UK and be in contact with local health and social services and University Medical Schools. Any discipline likes to see more money, but a good start could be made by rationalizing the use of existing funds. When so many promising centres are rendered inefficient and ineffective by uncertain financing and the need to do opportunistic research to survive, it is hard to justify the continued use of the responsive mode of research funding for one-off projects. The co-ordination of policy between the MRC, the Social Science Research Council and the Chief Scientist Organization could achieve a strategic plan for the continuation or establishment of a dozen strong centres specializing in particular fields but also undertaking some common tasks. Provided they possessed the degree of research autonomy given to Research Council Units, they could be sited within, alongside, or away from Universities.

I have felt the need to be as critical of Universities, of general sociology, and of their joint capacity to advance research in medical sociology as I was of some aspects of the health services. It is however a relative criticism based on membership, on recognition of remarkable advances in medical sociology during my professional career and of the quality and research sophistication of its practitioners. The subject is well established. The conditions of production, however, dictate the nature of the product and

174

instead of the conditions appropriate to a young proselytizing discipline it now needs the conditions for high quality volume output.

REFERENCES

AITKEN-SWAN, J. (1976) 'Epidemiological background', in HOROBIN, G. (ed.) *Experience with Abortion*. (London: Cambridge University Press).
— — (1977) *Fertility Control and the Medical Profession*. (London: Croom Helm).
ARBER, S. (1978) *Medical Sociology in Britain: a register of teaching and research*. (London: British Sociological Association).
ASKHAM, J. (1975) *Fertility and Deprivation*. (London: Cambridge University Press).
ATKINSON, P., DINGWALL, R. AND MURCOTT, A. (1979) *Prospects for the National Health*. (London: Croom Helm).
BAIRD, D. AND THOMSON, A. (1963), in BUTLER, N. AND ALBERMAN, E. (eds) *Perinatal Problems*. (London: Livingstone).
BARBER, B. (1962) 'Resistance by scientists to scientific discovery', in BARBER, B. AND HIRSCH, W. (eds) *The Sociology of Science*. (New York: Free Press).
BARNARD, K., LEE, K. AND REYNOLDS, J. (1977) *Tracing Decision-making in the NHS*. Report commissioned by the Royal Commission on the NHS.
BATTYE, G., BURDETT, F. AND SMITH, M. (1977) *Decision Tracking in the NHS*. Report commissioned by the Royal Commission on the NHS.
BAYLEY, M. (1973) *Mental Handicap and Community Care*. (London: Routledge and Kegan Paul).
BHATIA, J. (1971, 1973, 1974) Several articles in *Social Science and Medicine*. See **5**, 137–150; **17**, 507–16; and **9**, 15–21.
BINDER, A. (1964) 'Statistical theory', in FARNSWORTH, P., McNEMAR, O. AND McNEMAR, Q. (eds) *Annual Review of Psychology*, 1964, **15**, 277–310.
BLAXTER, M. (1976) *The Meaning of Disability*. (London: Heinemann).
— — (1978) 'Diagnosis as category and process: the case of alcoholism', *Soc. Sci. & Med.* **12**, 1a, 9–17.
— — (1980) *The Health of the Children: a review of research*. (London: Heinemann, in press).
— — AND PATERSON, E. (1980) *Attitudes to Health and use of Health Services (with special reference to children)* in *Two Generations of Women in Social Classes IV and V*. Report to DHSS/SSRC Joint Working Party on Transmitted Deprivation (in press).
BLOOR, M. (1980) *A Report on the Relationship between Informal Patient Interaction and the Formal Treatment Programme in a Day Hospital using Therapeutic Community Methods*. (Aberdeen: Institute of Medical Sociology, mimeo).
— — AND VENTERS, G. (1978) *An Epidemiological and Sociological Study of Variations in the Incidence of Operations on the Tonsils and Adenoids*. Occasional Paper No. 2. (Aberdeen: Institute of Medical Sociology).

References

— —, HOROBIN, G., TAYLOR, R. AND WILLIAMS, R. (1978) *Island Health Care: access to primary care in the Western Isles.* Occasional Paper No. 3. (Aberdeen: Institute of Medical Sociology).

— — AND VENTERS, G. (1980) Personal communication.

BREWERTON, D. AND DANIEL, J. (1971) 'Factors influencing return to work', *Br. med. J.* 4, 227–81.

BROWN, G. AND HARRIS, T. (1978) *Social Origins of Depression.* (London: Tavistock).

BROWN, R. (1979) *Reorganising the National Health Service.* (Oxford: Blackwell and Martin Robertson).

BULMER, M. (1977) *Sociological Research Methods.* (London: Macmillan).

BYRNE, P.S. AND LONG, B.E.L. (1976) *Doctors Talking to Patients.* (London: HMSO).

CARO, F. (1971) *Readings in Evaluative Research.* (New York: Russell Sage Foundation).

CARTWRIGHT, A. (1967) *Patients and their Doctors.* (London: Routledge and Kegan Paul).

CHALMERS, I. (1979) 'The search for indices', *Lancet*, ii, 1063–65.

CHAMBERLAIN, G. (1979) 'Background to perinatal health', *Lancet*, ii, 1061–63.

COATES, B. AND RAWSTRON, E. (1971) *Regional Variations in Britain.* (London: Batsford).

COCHRANE, A. (1972) *Effectiveness and Efficiency.* (London: Nuffield Provincial Hospitals Trust).

COMAROFF, J. (1976) 'Communicating information about non-fatal illness: the strategies of a group of general practitioners', *Sociol. Rev.* 24, 269.

CONRAD, P. (1979) 'Types of medical social control', *Sociol. Hlth. Illn.* I, 1–11.

COOK, T. AND CAMPBELL, D. (1979) *Quasi-experimentation: design and analysis issues in field settings.* (Chicago: Rand McNally).

COOPER, M. (1975) *Rationing Health Care.* (London: Croom Helm).

COSER, R. (1958) 'Authority and decision making in a hospital: a comparative analysis', *Am. Soc. Rev.* 23, 56–63.

CULYER, A. (1973) *The Economics of Social Policy.* (London: Martin Robertson).

— — (1976) *Need and the National Health Service.* (London: Martin Robertson).

— — AND WRIGHT, K. (eds) (1978) *Economic Aspects of Health Services.* (London: Martin Robertson).

DAHLSTRÖM, E. AND LILJESTRÖM, R. (1980) Personal communication.

DAVIES, C. AND FRANCIS, A. (1976) 'Perceptions of structure in NHS hospitals', in STACEY, M. (ed.) *The Sociology of the NHS.* (University of Keele).

DAVIES, P. (1979) 'Motivation, responsibility and sickness in the psychiatric treatment of alcoholism', *Br. J. Psychiat.* 134, 449–58.

DAVIS, A. (1979) 'An unequivocal change of policy: prevention health and medical sociology', *Soc. Sci. & Med.* 13a, 129–37.

— — AND HOROBIN, G. (1977) *Medical Encounters: the experience of illness and treatment.* (London: Croom Helm).

References

DAVIS, F. (1960) 'Uncertainty in medical prognosis: clinical and functional', *Am. J. Soc.* **66**, 41–47.

— — (1963) *Passage Through Crisis.* (Indianapolis: Bobbs Merrill).

DENZIN, N. (1970) *The Research Act in Sociology: a theoretical introduction to sociological methods.* (London: Butterworth).

DHSS (1976) *Sharing Resources for Health in England.* Report of the Resource Allocation Working Party. (London: HMSO).

— — (1976) *Prevention and Health: everybody's business.* (London: HMSO).

DOLLERY, C. (1978) *The End of an Age of Optimism.* (London: The Nuffield Provincial Hospitals Trust).

DOUGLAS, J. (1967) *The Social Meanings of Suicide.* (New Jersey: Princeton University Press).

DURKHEIM, E. (1897) *Suicide.* (London: 1951, Routledge and Kegan Paul: English translation of 1897 French edition).

ELINSON, J. (1972) 'Effectiveness of social action programs in health and welfare', in WEISS, C. *Evaluating Action Programs.* (Boston: Allyn and Bacon).

EVANS-PRITCHARD, E.E. (1937) *Witchcraft, Oracles and Magic among the Azande.* (Oxford: Clarendon Press).

FABREGA, H. (1974) *Disease and Social Behaviour: an interdisciplinary perspective.* (Cambridge, Mass.: M.I.T. Press).

FORSYTH, G. (1973) *Doctors and State Medicine.* (London: Pitman Medical).

FOX, R. (1957) 'Training for uncertainty', in MERTON, R.K. et al, (eds) *The Student-physician.* (Cambridge, Mass.: Harvard University Press).

— — (1959) *Experiment perilous.* (Glencoe, Ill.: Free Press).

— — (1976) 'The sociology of modern medical research', in LESLIE, C. (ed.) *Asian Medical Systems: a comparative study.* (Berkeley: University of California Press).

FRAKE, C.O. (1961) 'The diagnosis of disease among the Subanun of Mindanao', *Am. Anthr.* **62**, 113–22.

FREIDSON, E. (1970) *Professional Dominance: the social structure of medical care.* (New York: Atherton Press).

— — (1975) *Doctoring Together: a study of professional social control.* (New York: Elsevier).

FOWKES, F. (1980) 'Cholecystectomy and surgical resources in Scotland', *Hlth. Bull.* **38**, 126–31.

GILL, D. (1976) *The Growth, Development and Re-structuring of the British National Health Service.* (University of Missouri-Colombia: Section of Behavioural Sciences, School of Medicine, mimeo).

GLASER, R. AND STRAUSS, A. (1965) *Awareness of Dying.* (Chicago: Aldine Publishing Company).

GLOVER, J. (1938) 'The incidence of tonsillectomy in school children.', *Proc. R. Soc. Med.* **31**, 1219.

— — (1948) 'The paediatric approach to tonsillectomy', *Arch. Dis. Child.* **23**, 1.

GLUCKMAN, M. (1944) 'The logic of African science and witchcraft', *Rhodes-Livingstone Inst. J.*, 61–71.

References

GOLDIE, N. (1976) 'The division of labour among the mental health professions—a negotiated or an imposed order?' in STACEY et al (eds) *Health and the Division of Labour*. (London: Croom Helm).

HALL, M. AND CHNG, P. (1980) *An Appraisal of Out-patient Antenatal Care*. Report to Chief Scientist. (Scottish Home and Health Department).

HALL, P., LAND, H., PARKER, R. AND WEBB, A. (1975) *Change, Choice and Conflict in Social Policy*. (London: Heinemann).

HART, J. (1971) 'The inverse care law', *Lancet*, i, 405–12.

HART, N. (1978) *Health and Inequality*. (University of Essex: Department of Sociology, mimeo).

HAUSER, M. (ed.) (1972) *The Economics of Medical Care*. (London: Allen and Unwin).

HERZLICH, C. (1973) *Health and Illness*. (London: Academic Press).

HILL, D. (1978) 'Political ambiguity and policy: the case of welfare', *Soc. Econ. Admin.* **12**, 89–119.

HOROBIN, G. (forthcoming) 'Professional mystery: the maintenance of charisma in general medical practice', in DINGWALL, R. AND LEWIS, P. (eds) *The Sociology of the Professions: lawyers, doctors and others*. (London: Macmillan).

—— AND MCINTOSH, J. (1977) 'Responsibility in general practice', in STACEY, M. et al (eds) *Health and the Division of Labour*. (London: Croom Helm).

HUGHES, E. (1958) *Men and Their Work*. (Glencoe, Ill.: Free Press).

HUNTER, D. (1980) *Coping with Uncertainty: policy and politics in the National Health Service*. (London: Wiley, in press).

—— (1980a) Personal communication.

HYMAN, M. (1979) *Invalidity Pension*. Report to the DHSS (London School of Economics and Political Science).

ILLICH, I. (1975) *Medical Nemesis*. (London: Calder and Boyars).

ILLSLEY, R. (1955) 'Social class and selection and class differences in relation to stillbirths and infant deaths', *Br. med. J.* ii, 1520.

—— (1956a) *The Social Background to First Pregnancy*. (University of Aberdeen: PhD thesis).

—— (1956b) 'Duration of ante-natal care', *Med. Off.* **96**, 107.

—— AND TAYLOR, R. (1974) *Sociological Aspects of Teenage Pregnancy*. Occasional Paper No. 1. (Aberdeen: Institute of Medical Sociology).

—— (1975) 'Promotion to observer status', *Soc. Sci. & Med.* **9**, 63–7.

—— (1976) 'Developments in the role of medicine in reproduction', in SOKOLOWSKA, M. et al (eds) *Health, Medicine and Society*. (Warsaw: Polish Scientific Publishers).

—— AND GILL, D. (1968) 'Changing trends in illegitimacy', *Soc. Sci. & Med.* **2**, 415–33.

—— AND HALL, M. (1976) 'Psychosocial aspects of abortion', *Bull. WHO*, **53**, 83–106.

JEFFERYS, M. (1976) 'Social science teaching in medical education: an overview of the situation in Great Britain', in SOKOLOWSKA, M. et al (eds) *Health, Medicine and Society*. (Warsaw: Polish Scientific Publishers).

References

JOHNSON, G. AND JOHNSON, R. (1973) 'Paraplegics in Scotland: a survey of employment and facilities', *Br. J. Soc. W.* **3**, 1, 28–37.

—— (1977) 'Social services support for multiple sclerosis patients in West of Scotland', *Lancet*, **i**, 31–3.

JOHNSON, T. (1972) *Professions and Power*. (London: Macmillan).

KAPLAN, A. (1964) *The Conduct of Inquiry*. (San Francisco: Chandler Publishing Co.).

KEEBLE, U. (1979) *Aids and Adaptations*. Occasional papers in Social Administration No. 62. (London School of Economics and Political Science).

KLEIN, R. (1973) *Complaints Against Doctors: a study in professional accountability*. (London: Charles Knight).

—— (ed.) (1975) *Social policy and public expenditure 1975: inflation and priorities*. (London: Centre for Studies in Social Policy).

—— (1976a) 'Power, democracy and the NHS', *Br. med. J.* 1352–53.

—— (1976b) 'A policy for change', *Br. med. J.*, 353–4.

—— (1976c) 'Accountability in the NHS: whose head on the block?' *Br. med. J.* 1211–12.

KOGAN, M. et al (1978) *The working of the National Health Service*. Research Paper No. 1, Royal Commission on the National Health Service. (London: HMSO).

KOOS, E. (1954) *The Health of Regionville*. (New York: Columbia University Press).

LAST, J. (1963) 'The iceberg: completing the clinical picture in general practice', *Lancet*, **ii**, 28–31.

LAYTON, T. (1914) 'Tonsils and adenoids in children: a plea for fewer operations', *Trans. Med. Soc. Lond.* **27**, 244.

LEE, R. (1975) 'Medical rehabilitation: policy-making in the English health service', *Soc. Sci. & Med.* **9**, 325–32.

LESLIE, C. (1976) *Asian Medical Systems: a comparative study*. (Berkeley: University of California Press).

LEWIS, G. (1976) 'A view of sickness in New Guinea', in LOUDON, J.B. (ed.) *Social Anthropology and Medicine*. (London: Academic Press).

LIEBAN, R. (1976) 'Traditional medical beliefs and the choice of practitioners in a Philippine city', *Soc. Sci. & Med.* **10**, 6, 289–96.

LINDBLOM, C. (1959) 'The science of muddling through', *Publ. Admin.* **19**, 79–99.

McINTOSH, J. (1977) *Communication and Awareness in a Cancer Ward*. (London: Croom Helm).

MACINTYRE, S. (1976a) 'Who wants babies? the social construction of instincts', in BARKER, D. AND ALLEN, S. (eds) *Sexual Divisions in Society*. (London: Tavistock).

—— (1976b) 'To have or to have not: promotion and prevention of childbirth in gynaecological work', in STACEY, M. (ed.) *Sociology of the NHS*. (University of Keele).

References

—— (1977) *Single and Pregnant*. (London: Croom Helm).

—— (1980) in 'Needs and expectations in obstetrics', *Hlth. Bull.* **38**, 114.

McKINLAY, J. (1979) 'Epidemiological and political determinants of social policies regarding the public health', *Soc. Sci. & Med.* **13a**, 541–8.

McKEOWN, T. (1976) *The Role of Medicine: dream, mirage, or nemesis.* (London: The Nuffield Provincial Hospitals Trust).

MACLEAN, U. (1971) *Magical Medicine: a Nigerian case study.* (Oxford: Pergamon Press).

McPHERSON, K., EPSTEIN, A., STRONG, P. AND JONES, L. *Regional Variations in the Use of Common Surgical Procedures: within and between England and Wales, Canada and the United States of America.* (In press).

MARRIS, P. AND REIN, M. (1967) *Dilemmas of Social Reform.* (London: Routledge and Kegan Paul).

MECHANIC, D. (1971) 'The English National Health Service: some comparisons with the United States', *J. Hlth. and Soc. Beh.* **12**, 18–29.

—— (1974) *Politics, Medicine and Social Science.* (New York: Wiley).

—— (1976) *The Growth of Bureaucratic Medicine.* (New York: Wiley).

MILLS, C.W. (1959) *The Sociological Imagination.* (New York: Oxford University Press).

MOONEY, G., RUSSELL, E. AND WEIR, R. (1980) *Choices for Health Care.* (London: Macmillan).

MORONEY, R. (1976) *The Family and the State.* (Harlow: Longman).

MORRICE, J. AND TAYLOR, R. (1978) 'The intermittent husband syndrome', *New Society*, 5 January.

MORRIS, J. AND HEADY, J. (1955) 'Social and biological factors in infant mortality: V. Mortality in relation to father's occupation, 1911–1950', *Lancet*, **i**, 555–59.

NAJMAN, J. (1980) 'Theories of disease causation and the concept of a general susceptibility', *Soc. Sci. & Med.* **14a**, 231–37.

NATIONAL CORPORATION FOR THE CARE OF OLD PEOPLE (1979) *Organising Aftercare.* (London: National Corporation for the Care of Old People).

NAVARRO, V. (1977) *Medicine under Capitalism.* (London: Croom Helm).

NORTON, A. AND ROGERS, S. (1977) *Experiences of Collaboration.* Paper presented to a seminar on Collaboration between Local Government and the NHS organized by Nuffield Provincial Hospitals Trust, London.

—— —— (1977) *Collaboration between Health Authorities and Local Authorities: interim report.* (Birmingham: Institute of Local Government Studies, mimeo).

—— —— (1980) *The Health Service and Local Government Services: can they work together to meet the needs of the elderly and of other disadvantaged groups?* (Birmingham: Institute of Local Government Studies, mimeo).

OAKLEY, A. (1979) *Becoming a Mother.* (Oxford: Martin Robertson).

—— (1980) *Women Confined: towards a sociology of childbirth.* (Oxford: Martin Robertson).

References

OFFICE OF POPULATION CENSUSES AND SURVEYS (1978) *Occupational Mortality: decennial supplement 1970–1972*. (London: HMSO).

OSOFSKY, H.J. (1968) 'The walls are within: an exploration of barriers between middle-class physicians and poor patients', in DEUTSCHER, I.'AND THOMPSON, E.J. (eds) *Among the People: encounters with the poor*. (New York: Basic Books).

OWEN, D. (1976) *In Sickness and Health: the politics of medicine*. (London: Quartet).

PARSONS, T. (1958) 'Definitions of health and illness in light of American values and social structure', in JACO, E. (ed.) *Patients, Physicians and Illness*. (New York: Free Press).

POSNER, T. (1977) 'Magical elements in orthodox medicine', in DINGWALL, R., HEATH, C., REID, M. AND STACEY, M. (eds) *Health Care and Health Knowledge*. (London: Croom Helm).

PRESS, I. (1969) 'Urban illness: physicians, curers, and dual use in Bogota', *J. Hlth & Soc. Behav.* **10**, 3, 209–18.

POWLES, J. (1973) 'On the limitations of modern medicine', *Soc. Med. Man.* **1**, 1–30.

RAINWATER, L. (1960) *And the Poor get Children*. (Chicago: Quadrangle Books).

— — (1968) 'The lower class: health, illness and medical institutions', in DEUTSCHER, I. AND THOMPSON, E. (eds) *Among the People: Encounters with the Poor*. (New York: Basic Books).

RATOFF, L., ROSE, A. AND SMITH, C. (1974) 'Social workers and general practitioners—some problems of working together', *J. Roy. Coll. Gen. Practit.* **24**, 750–60.

REGISTRAR GENERAL, SCOTLAND. *Annual Reports*. (Edinburgh: HMSO).

REILLY, P., PATTEN, M. AND MOFFETT, J. (1977). 'Communications between doctors and social workers in a general practice', *J. Roy. Coll. Gen. Practit.* **27**, 289–93.

REIN, M. (1976) *Social Science and Public Policy*. (Harmondwsorth: Penguin).

RICHMON, J. AND GOLDTHORP, W. (1977) When was your last period? in DINGWALL, R. et al (eds), *Health Care and Health Knowledge*. (London: Croom Helm).

ROBINSON, D. (1977) *Self-help and health*. (London: Martin Robertson).

— — (1973) *Patients, Practitioners and Medical Care*. (London: Heinemann).

ROTH, J. (1957) 'Ritual and marriage in the control of contagion', *Am. Soc. Res.* **22**, no. 3.

— — (1963) *Time-tables*. (Indianapolis: Bobbs-Merrill).

— — (1974) 'Professionalism: the sociologist's decoy', *Soc. Wk. Occup.* **1**, 6–23.

ROYAL COMMISSION ON THE DISTRIBUTION OF THE INDUSTRIAL POPULATION (1940) *Report*. (London: HMSO).

RUBE, I.A. AND SPICER, E. (1977) *Ethnic Medicine in the South West*. (Tucson: University of Arizona Press).

References

SALTER, B. (1980) 'Cutting into the muscle of university research', *The Times Higher Education Supplement*, 397, 6 June 1980.

SCAMMELS, B. (1971) *The Administration of Health and Welfare Services*. (Manchester: University Press).

SCHWARTZ, H. AND JACOBS, J. (1979) *Qualitative Sociology*. (New York: Free Press).

SKEET, M. (1974) *Home from Hospital*. (London: Macmillan Journals).

SMITH, G. (1980) *Social Need*. (London: Routledge and Kegan Paul).

SOROKIN, P. (1959) *Social and Cultural Mobility*. (Glencoe, Ill.: Free Press).

SMITH, G. AND MAY, D. (1980) 'The artificial debate between rationalist and incrementalist models of decision-making', *Policy and Politics*. (In press).

STACEY, M. (ed.) (1976) *The Sociology of the NHS*. (University of Keele).

— — et al (1976) *Health and the Division of Labour*. (London: Croom Helm).

STACEY, N. AND FORSYTH, M. (1976) *Limitations in co-operation between Health and Local Authorities*. Paper presented to a seminar on Collaboration between Local Government and the NHS organized by Nuffield Provincial Hospitals Trust, London.

STEVENSON, N. (1980) Editorial Comment, *Soc. Sci. & Med.* **146**, 1.

STIMSON, G. AND WEBB, B. (1975) *Going to see the Doctor: the consultation process in general practice*. (London: Routledge and Kegan Paul).

— — (1976) 'General practitioners, "trouble", and types of patients', in STACEY, M. (ed.) *Sociology of the NHS*. (University of Keele).

STRAUS, R. (1978) 'Medical education and the doctor-patient relationship', in *The Doctor-patient Relationship in the Changing Health Service*. (Washington D.C.: Department of Health, Education, and Welfare).

STRONG, P. (1979) 'Sociological imperialism and the profession of medicine', *Soc. Sci. & Med.* **13a**, 199–215.

— — (1980) *The Ceremonial Order of the Clinic*. (London: Routledge and Kegan Paul).

STRUENING, E. AND GUTTENTAG, M. (1975) *Handbook of Evaluative Research Vol. 1*. (Beverley Hills: Sage Publications).

SUCHMAN, E. (1967) *Evaluative Research*. (New York: Russell Sage Foundation).

TAYLOR, R. (1977) 'The local health system: an ethnography of interest-groups and decision-making', *Soc. Sci. & Med.* **11**, 583–92.

— — (forthcoming) 'Self-reports and self-estimates of health', in BROTHERSTON, J. (ed.) *Planning and Provision of Services for the Elderly*. (Edinburgh: Churchill-Livingstone).

THOMPSON, B. (1956) 'Social study of illegitimate maternities', *Br. J. prev. soc. Med.* **10**, 75.

— — AND AITKEN-SWAN, J. (1973) 'Pregnancy outcome and fertility control in Aberdeen', *Brit. J. prev. soc. Med.* **27**, 3, 137–45.

TITMUSS, R. (1943) *Birth, Poverty and Wealth*. (London: Hamish Hamilton).

— — (1970) *The gift relationship*. (London: Allen and Unwin).

TOWNSEND, P. (1979) *Poverty in the United Kingdom*. (Harmondsworth: Penguin Books).

References

VOYSEY, M. (1975) *A Constant Burden*. (London: Routledge and Kegan Paul).

WADSWORTH, M., BUTTERFIELD, W. AND BLANCY, R. (1971) *Health and Sickness: the choice of treatment*. (London: Tavistock).

WALTERS, V. (1980) *Class Inequality and Health Care*. (London: Croom Helm).

WARNER, K. (1979) 'The economic implications of preventive health care', *Soc. Sci. & Med.* **13c**, 227–37.

WEBB, A. AND HOBDELL, M. (1980) 'Co-ordination and teamwork in the health and personal social srvices' in LONSDALE, S., WEBB, A. AND BRIGGS, T. (eds) *Teamwork in the personal social services and health care*. (London: Croom Helm).

WEBB, E., CAMPBELL, D., SCHWARTZ, R. AND SECHREST, L. (1966) *Unobtrusive Measures: non-reactive research in the social sciences*. (Chicago: Rand McNally)

WEISS, C. (1972) *Evaluating Action Programs*. (Boston: Allyn and Bacon).

WEST, P. (1977) 'Geographical variations in mortality from ischaemic heart disease in England and Wales; *Brit. J. prev. soc. Med.* **31**, 245–50.

WESTERGAARD, J. AND RESLER, H. (1975) *Class in a Capitalist Society*. (London: Heinemann).

WILLIAMS, A. AND ANDERSON, R. (1975) *Efficiency in the Social Services*. (London: Martin Robertson).

WILLIAMSON, D. AND DARAHER, K. (1978) *Self-care in Health*. (London: Croom Helm).

WINSLOW, C.A. (1967) *The Conquest of Epidemic Disease*. (New York: Hafner).

WISEMAN, C. (1978) 'Selection of major planning issues', *Pol. Sci.* **9**.

—— (1979) 'Strategic planning in the Scottish NHS—a mixed-scanning approach', *Long Range Planning*, April.

WYNN, M. AND WYNN, A. (1979) *Prevention of Handicap and the Health of Women*. (London: Routledge and Kegan Paul).

ZOLA, I. (1972) 'Medicine as an institution of social control', *Sociol. Rev.* **20**, 487–504.